Carry On, Warrior

The real truth about being a woman

GLENNON MELTON

PENGUIN BOOKS

PENGUIN BOOKS

Published by the Penguin Group
Penguin Books Ltd, 80 Strand, London WC2R 0RL, England
Penguin Group (USA) Inc., 375 Hudson Street, New York, New York 10014, USA
Penguin Group (Canada), 90 Eglinton Avenue East, Suite 700, Toronto, Ontario, Canada M4P 2Y3
(a division of Pearson Penguin Canada Inc.)
Penguin Ireland, 25 St Stephen's Green, Dublin 2, Ireland (a division of Penguin Books Ltd)
Penguin Group (Australia), 707 Collins Street, Melbourne, Victoria 3008, Australia
(a division of Pearson Australia Group Pty Ltd)
Penguin Books India Pvt Ltd, 11 Community Centre, Panchsheel Park, New Delhi – 110 017, India
Penguin Group (NZ), 67 Apollo Drive, Rosedale, Auckland 0632, New Zealand
(a division of Pearson New Zealand Ltd)
Penguin Books (South Africa) (Pty) Ltd, Block D, Rosebank Office Park,
181 Jan Smuts Avenue, Parktown North, Gauteng 2193, South Africa

Penguin Books Ltd, Registered Offices: 80 Strand, London WC2R 0RL, England

www.penguin.com

First published in the USA by Scribner, an imprint of Simon & Schuster Inc. 2013
First published in Great Britain by Penguin Books 2013
001

Lyrics on page 111 from 'Hallelujah' © Sony/ATV Music Publishing, LLC, 1985
All rights administered by Sony/ATV Music Publishing, LLC

Excerpt from 'On Self-Respect' from *Slouching Towards Bethlehem*
by Joan Didion © Joan Didion, 1966, 1968, renewed 1996
Reprinted by permission of Farrar, Straus and Giroux, LLC and by permission of the author

Carry On, Warrior contains essays previously published on momastery.com as well as new material

Certain names and identifying characteristics have been changed and certain
characters and events have been reordered or compressed

Typeset by Jouve (UK), Milton Keynes
Printed in England by Clays Ltd, St Ives plc

ISBN: 978-0-718-17736-2

www.greenpenguin.co.uk

ALWAYS LEARNING   **PEARSON**

Dedication

One night my mom, Tisha, was visiting and she asked to talk to me privately. She looked nervous. We walked into my bedroom and leaned up against the bed pillows together. We talked, slowly and carefully, about my writing. She told me how beautiful she thought it was and how hard it was for her to read. She described the pain she felt when she read about my secret life and how confused she was that it all happened while we did our very best to love each other. We talked about how scary it is to share these stories with friends and strangers.

We cried a little and laughed a little, too. But they were teary laughs.

We talked for a long time, and then it felt as if we were almost done. I was sad, because I wanted to stay on that bed with my mom forever. I thought about that in the quiet for a while. I wondered what she was thinking. Then my mom looked at me and her lip quivered and even though she was very, very scared she said, *I am so proud of you. I am in awe of what you and God have done together. You have to tell your stories. This is what you were meant to do. Don't stop telling your stories, Honey.*

It was like when I told her I was pregnant, and she was very, very scared, but she looked straight at me and said, *Glennon, you don't have to marry him if you don't want to. We can raise the baby together. We can handle this.*

It was like when my baby sister, Amanda, announced she was moving to Africa to save little girls from an epidemic of child rape. And even though my mom was very, very scared, she eventually said, *It's what you need to do. Go.*

People are always calling my mom an angel, but I think she is a warrior.

And I want her to know that this book, and every single word that I write, is for her.

"Be kind, for everyone you meet is fighting a hard battle."
—Rev. John Watson

"Including you."
—Glennon

Contents

Contents

MULTIPLYING

Contents

HOLDING ON

LETTING GO

Cast of Characters

Like yours, my story is tough to categorize. My life is a tragedy, comedy, romance, adventure, or redemption story depending on the decade, time of day, and how much sleep I've had. The constant in my story—the river that runs through it—is my cast of characters.

My husband, Craig, volunteers to help friends move before they ask. He dances in the kitchen, bathroom, and grocery store. He plays hide and seek with our dog, Theo, when the kids get tired of playing. He remains calm. He wakes every two hours to check our kids' fevers when they're sick. He holds his tongue and my friends' crying babies. He's golden. And broken. Just like me.

My firstborn, Chase, is the one who changed everything, just by being born.

My girls, Tish and Amma, mostly scare me. How do I raise little girls before I'm finished raising my own little girl self?

My Sister, Amanda, is my Lobster and my left lung. How I breathed without her for the first three years of my life remains a mystery. Sister's husband, John, is my safety deposit box. I trust him to hold and protect my most precious treasure.

My dad, Bubba, translates his love and wisdom into words, like me. My mama, Tisha, translates her love and wisdom into actions, like Craig.

Cast of Characters

I'll add God to my cast of characters. I can't explain him or her at all, because I don't understand his ways. I just know he's the one who cast these folks in my story. I'm grateful.

CARRY ON, WARRIOR

Building a Life

A few years ago, strange things started happening to me at church. I'd find myself in the middle of a lighthearted conversation with a woman I'd just met, and the woman would make a joke that didn't sound like a joke, suggesting that our family was "perfect" and that this "perfection" made her feel bad about her own family. This happened three or four times over a two-week period. Once a woman said, "You are so *pulled together*. It makes me feel so *apart*."

My husband, Craig, was standing next to me at the time, and I looked at him confused while he looked back at me, equally confused. This is our signature interaction. I stammered my way through the rest of the conversation, and on the way home Craig and I debriefed.

We were baffled. Craig and I adore each other, but neither of us would describe the other as "pulled together." These women may as well have been saying to me, "I'm just so jealous of your *height* and *culinary genius*." I'm five two *and a half*, and all I know of cooking is how to make the call that results in the delivery of dinner. During our debriefing, Craig and I developed a theory that if you are thin and smile a lot, people tend to believe that you have the universe's secrets in your pocket and that a raindrop has never fallen on your head. If you also happen to be wearing trendy jeans, well then, *fuggedaboutit*.

This theory distressed me greatly. I do not like to make other women feel less than. And I wanted my insides and outsides to match somehow. But I was scared I'd have to start looking like Pig Pen or Courtney Love to make that happen. You see, I'm a recovering bulimic and alcoholic. For twenty years, I was lost to food and booze and bad love and drugs. I suffered. My family suffered.

I had a relatively magical childhood, which added an extra layer of guilt to my pain and confusion. *Glennon—why are you all jacked up when you have no excuse to be all jacked up?* My best guess is that I was born a little broken, with an extra dose of sensitivity. Growing up, I felt that I was missing the layer of protection I needed to expose myself to life's risks—risks like friendship, tender love, and rejection. I felt awkward, unworthy, and vulnerable. And I didn't want to walk through life's battlefield feeling that way. I didn't think I'd survive. So I made up my own little world called addiction and I hid there. I felt safe. No one could touch me.

Then that changed. On Mother's Day, 2002, unwed and addicted, I discovered I was pregnant. I alternated between staring at the test in my shaking hand and into my bloodshot eyes in the bathroom mirror. I tried to force these truths to mesh: I am a drunk. I am alone. I am pregnant.

And because I had no clue what else to do, I prayed. I prayed the only way I know how to pray—in moans and accusations and apologies and tears and wild promises. When I finally stood up from the bathroom floor, I decided to become a mother. I walked out of the bathroom and vowed to never again have another drink, cigarette, drug, unhealthy relationship, or food binge. That vow has been hard to keep. In a whirlwind, I found myself married to a man I'd known for ten sober nights. Marrying Craig turned out to be the best decision I never really made.

During that time, I discovered that I was strong. That was the first true thing I ever learned about myself. I also learned that wifedom, motherhood, and sober life were really quite difficult. I always wondered if other women found these things to be as difficult as I did.

Then, one day I was at the playground with a new friend from church named Tess. I suspected that Tess was having trouble in her marriage. We hadn't talked about this, though, because we were too busy talking about more important things, like soccer practice and highlights. I felt frustrated that our conversation never went deeper. We seemed incapable of discussing the very things that were most important to discuss.

Lost in my frustration, I started thinking about all the time and effort I'd spent building protective layers between my broken heart and the broken world. I considered the ways I'd distanced myself from other people—people who might hurt me more than I was already hurting. People who might be disgusted if they saw the real me. My fear of really being seen had driven me to hide inside the bunker of addiction for decades. When I finally crawled out, I pulled on my secrets and shame like armor and carried my invulnerability like a weapon. Life, to me, had always seemed like a battle to survive. But there at the playground, I realized that surviving wasn't enough anymore. Sitting there with Tess, I realized I wasn't really *sitting there with Tess at all*. There were so many layers of my armor and her armor between us that we couldn't touch each other. And even if we'd wanted to, we couldn't have gotten close enough because we were shooting at each other with stories about our "perfect" lives.

Suddenly this all seemed completely ridiculous. Sure, I was sober and out of hiding, but by denying my past to others, protecting myself with the shield of secrets and shame, I had isolated myself. I was lonely, and a bit bored. Life without touching other people is boring as hell. It hit me that maybe the battles of life are best fought *without* armor and *without* weapons. That maybe life gets real, good, and interesting when we remove all of the layers of protection we've built around our hearts and walk out onto the battlefield of life *naked*. I wondered, *If I put down my guns, will Tess do the same?* I decided it was a worthy experiment.

I shed my armor and I waved my white flag. All of a sudden I heard myself saying the following to Tess:

Listen. I want you to know that I'm a recovering alcohol, drug, and food addict. I've been arrested because of those things. Craig and I got accidentally pregnant and married a year after we started dating. We love each other madly, but I'm secretly terrified that our issues with sex and anger will eventually screw things up. Sometimes I feel sad and worried when good things happen to other people. I snap at customer service people and my kids and husband regularly. I always have rage right beneath my surface. And right now I'm dealing with postpartum depression. I spend most of my day wishing my kids would just leave me alone. Chase brought me a note the other morning that said, "I hope Mommy is nice today." It's depressing and scary, because I keep wondering what will happen if that feeling never goes away. Maybe I can't handle this mommy thing. Anyway, I wanted to let you know.

Tess stared at me for so long that I wondered if she was going to call our minister or 911. Then I saw some tears dribble down her cheek. We sat there, and she told me everything. Things with her husband were bad, apparently. Really bad. Tess felt scared and alone. But at the playground that day, Tess decided she wanted help and love more than she wanted me to think she was perfect.

We hardly knew each other, but we both realized that we were in this together. We went through some tough times over the next few months. Therapy, separation, anger, fear, and lots of tears. But a little army of love circled the wagons around Tess and her family and blockaded anybody from getting too far in or out. And eventually things got better. Tess, her husband, and their beautiful children are together and healing and thriving now. And I got to watch all of that. I actually got to see the truth set a family free.

At that point in my life, I was dying to do something meaningful and helpful outside of my home, but no one would have me. We were rejected again and again when we tried to adopt. Then I tried to become a volunteer at the local nursing home. They seemed thrilled with me until the background check. They never called back. Perhaps they thought I had a secret motivation to get all the old people wasted. Then I tried to volunteer at a local shelter for survivors of domestic violence. It looked as if they might have me until the final interview, when the woman said, "As a formality, I just have to ask if you've ever been arrested." It was hard to explain that it was *only five times*. She never called me back, either.

I was depressed.

But then the Tess thing happened. And I thought, Maybe I could do *that*. Maybe my public service could be to tell people the truth about my insides. It struck me that for this particular "ministry," *my criminal record was a plus*. It gave me street cred. And I considered that maybe the gifts God gave me were storytelling and shamelessness. Because I *am* shameless. I'm almost ashamed at how little shame I have. Almost, but not really at all.

So I decided that's what God wanted me to do. He wanted me

to walk around telling people the truth. No mask, no hiding, no pretending. That was going to be *my thing*. I was going to make people feel better about their insides by showing them mine. By being my real self. But I was keeping my trendy jeans. I decided they were part of my real self.

A few days after I told Craig that I was going to "volunteer" as a "reckless truth teller," my minister called me on the phone. My first thought was that Tess had ratted me out. But the minister said, "I know you're having a hard time with the baby, and it might seem like a bad idea, but you need to tell your story to the church. The whole church. On stage. Live." Craig sweated and looked into whether he could be fired for having an ex-con for a wife. I planned my outfit.

Then I wrote down my story, without leaving anything out. I read it to my church, and it went really, really well. People were shocked. It is so fun to shock people. Lots and lots of people wanted to cry with me and tell me their stories. And I thought, *Okay, then. Take **that**, nursing home. I didn't want to serve your stupid lemonade anyway. Does one get standing ovations and tears of joy for serving lemonade? I think **not**.*

I'd found my thing: openness. I decided, based on firsthand experience, that it was more fun to say things that made other women feel hopeful about themselves and God than it was to say or omit things to make people feel jealous of me. And it was easier too. Less to keep track of and monitor.

I started writing a few months later, so that I could tell my truth recklessly to more people. After reading a few of my essays, my dad, Bubba, called and said, "Glennon. *Don't you think there are some things you should take to the grave?*" I thought hard for a moment and said, "No. I really **don't**. That sounds *horrible* to me. I don't want to take *anything* to the grave. I want to die used up and emptied out. I don't want to carry around anything that I don't have to. I want to travel light."

When I got sober, I woke up and stepped out into real life for the first time. I was twenty-six years old, but because I'd been in hiding since I was eight, I saw the world through the eyes of a child. I was awed and afraid. My heart opened to the world's beauty and brutality. I looked closely at humanity and all of its brokenness and decided to forgive it and myself. Since brokenness is the way of folks, the only way to live peacefully is to forgive everyone constantly, including yourself. I decided that I had nothing to be ashamed of. I'd done the best I could with what I had. I'd do better now. Mostly.

This new-found state of forgiveness and hope allowed me to trust another human being with my whole heart, so I got married. It became clear that marriage was hard and holy work. I learned that I could do hard things. I learned I was worthy and capable of being another human being's constant. And this confidence helped me widen my circles. I had Chase, Tish, and Amma. I became an active part of my community. And I reached out to God: the ultimate circle—the One that holds us all together.

I realized that these widening circles—accepting myself, my partner, my children, my community, and my faith—were the only layers of protection I needed. These circles were my life, and I was at the center: naked and honest and sober and broken and imperfectly perfect. A work of art in constant progress.

The more I opened my heart to the folks in my circles, the more convinced I became that life is equal parts brutal and beautiful. And/Both. Life is *brutiful*. Like stars in a dark sky. Sharing life's brutiful is what makes us feel less alone and afraid. The truth can't be stuffed down with food or booze or exercise or work or cutting or shopping for long. Hiding from the truth causes its own unique pain, and it's lonely pain. Life is hard—not because we're doing it wrong, just because it's hard. It's okay to talk, write, paint, or cry about that. It helps.

This book is my story, and I hope it's yours too. It's about how I built my circles—how I built a life—and what it means to me to carry on.

WAKING UP

Sisters

My decision to get sober was more like a weary surrender than a bold march into battle. After I had allowed my life to fall into a thousand pieces for the thousandth time, Bubba and Tisha planned a loving intervention. Then I found out I was pregnant with Chase, and I realized that I was running out of people and options. At the time, the path of least resistance seemed to be sobriety.

It's not somebody who's seen the light
It's a cold and it's a broken hallelujah.

I called my sister and said, "Sister, do the thing you always do," which is to figure out what the hell happens next, and then make that thing happen. A few hours later, she gathered up my broken self and we drove to our first AA meeting.

Sister held my sweaty, shaky hand and walked just in front of me, scanning for problems or people from whom to shield me, like she always does. She took an AA brochure from a table so we'd have something to look down at when we sat and joined the circle. On the front was a list of alcoholism warning signs:

Do you drink more than four servings in a setting?
One time I didn't.

11

Do you ever drink in the mornings?
Only on weekends.
Do you ever black out?
Can't remember.
Have you suffered negative consequences from drinking?
Being here seems like a pretty negative consequence.

Neither of us said a word until my sister leaned over and whispered, "I don't know if AA is going to be sufficient. We might need Triple A."

After the meeting, we came home, sat on my bed together, and stared at the disaster on my bedroom floor. During my drinking decades, I lived like a pig. My room was a hazardous pile of stilettos, tube tops, wine bottles, ashtrays, and old magazines. I valued nothing. Everything that came into my life was disposable: clothes, opportunities, people. My bedroom looked as if my insides had spilled out onto the floor.

After a few minutes of quiet, Sister climbed down from the bed and started picking things up, one piece of trash at a time. She threw away the wine bottles and the cigarettes, she folded the tube tops, and she gently tossed the magazines. I watched for a while and then joined her. We hung up every piece of clothing, wiped down every gritty surface, poured out every hidden bottle of booze. We worked silently, side by side, for two hours. Then we sat back down on my bed and held hands. My room looked so different. It looked like a place where a girl might want to live. I wondered if my head and my heart might one day be places I'd like to live too.

It was the beginning.

Holy Holes

Life is a quest to find an unfindable thing.

This is the problem. Life is a bit of a setup. We are put here needing something that doesn't exist here. And that, as my friend Adrianne says, is *some bullshit*.

The writer Anne Lamott (St. Anne) calls this unquenchable thirst our "God-sized hole." People of faith believe that God put us here yearning for what will only be found in heaven: him. I get that, sort of, but it still seems a bit twisted to me. What if I put my daughter Amma in a playpen with her pacifier dangling just out of her reach? What is the point of this life if we can't have what we need? What are we to do with our God-sized holes in the meantime, before we die? How are we ever supposed to be comfortable down here with a big old hole in the middle of our hearts?

Since I'm a slow learner, I tried to fill mine with poisonous things for twenty years.

When I was very, very young, I started trying to fill myself with food. Food was my comfort, refuge, and joy. Food was my God. But then I realized that my emptiness was also the need for beauty. I thought that beauty meant being thin and dressing right. Of course, those things don't have a lot to do with beauty, but, as I said, I was young.

Since I didn't believe I was beautiful, I wanted to hide. But when you're a kid, there's no hiding. You have to go where they tell you to go, looking how you look, wearing what you're wearing. So every day, I was pushed out the door, all imperfect and greasy and roly-poly for everyone to see. Showing up just as you are seemed a ridiculous thing to ask of someone so young. I decided that if I had to be so visible, I needed to shrink.

But how do you fill yourself with thinness when you also need to fill yourself with food?

I learned the answer when I was eight from a TV movie about bulimia. The film was created to be a warning, but I accepted it as a gift. Here was a way to fill up, to allow myself to continue using food for comfort and escape without paying any consequences. After the movie, I binged and purged for the first time. Bulimia made me comfortable because when I was in the midst of a binge, I lost consciousness of my discomfort and my emptiness. When the purge was over, though, and I lay exhausted on the bathroom floor, my hole felt even bigger. That's how you can tell that you're filling yourself with the wrong things. You use a lot of energy, and in the end, you feel emptier and less comfortable than ever.

Bulimia was hard, but it was easier than real life. I felt safer there in my own little dramatic food world. So I dropped out of life and into Bulimia. For almost twenty years, I binged and purged several times each day. Fill the hole, empty the hole. I didn't come back to life until I was twenty-six. But life went on anyway, as it does.

One night in seventh grade, I slept over at my friend Susie's house, and we snuck out to a high school party. It was the first time I'd ever had a beer, and I drank so many that I blacked out completely. I don't remember being at the party, but I was later told that some seniors tried to microwave my hands. After the party, I slept at Susie's and threw up all night. The following day, I called my mom to tell her I had the flu and she needed to pick me up. She was sympathetic. I was hooked. Beer: another way to become unconscious, to drop out of life a little bit more. I quickly became an alcoholic because of bad genes and the fact that you can never get enough of what you don't need.

I spent time in a mental hospital during my senior year of high school. I'd been a bulimic for nine years, and therapy wasn't helping, especially since I spent my sessions discussing how fine I was and wasn't the weather just lovely? Then one random Wednesday, I ate too much at lunch and thought I was going to die. To me, full equaled death. But I couldn't find a place to throw up. So finally, right there in the middle of the senior hallway, I decided I was **not fine**, not at all. I walked into my guidance counselor's office and said: "Call my parents. I need to be hospitalized. I can't handle anything. Someone needs to help me."

I was a student government officer to a class of close to a thousand. An athlete too. Relatively pretty. Smart. Seemingly confident. My Senior Superlative was "Leading Leader." I was nominated for homecoming court and hosted pep rallies for four thousand classmates. People who need help sometimes look a lot like people who don't need help.

That high school counselor called my parents, and they came right away. They found a place for me to get help. I often think about what that day must have been like for them. Maybe they desperately wanted to say: *No, no it will be okay! Not a hospital! We are your parents! We can fix this!* But they didn't. The moment I became brave enough to admit I needed help, they believed me, and despite the shock, pain, and stigma, they gave me the exact help I requested.

There weren't many eating disorder clinics back then, so I

went to a real mental hospital. There were only two of us in the unit with eating issues. The others were there because they were schizophrenic, drug addicted, depressed, or suicide risks. Many of the patients had violent tendencies. I do not remember being afraid of any of them. I do remember being afraid, in one way or another, of everyone in my high school.

There was art therapy and dance therapy and group therapy. It all made sense to me. The things the other patients said made sense to me, even though they weren't things that my peers in real life would have ever, ever said. There were rules about how to listen well and how to respond. There were lessons about how to empathize and where to find the courage to speak. I enjoyed these lessons much more than my high school classes. They seemed important. We learned how to care about ourselves and about each other.

I trembled the morning of my release. I knew I wasn't ready, but that I had to go anyway, because I would never be ready. Inside the hospital was so much easier and safer and surer than outside the hospital. Life made sense to me in there. On the outside, it seemed every man was for himself.

I did leave, though. We all had to.

I graduated from high school and went off to college, where I added pot to my list of hole-filling strategies. That did not go well either. My friends and I would sit down and start smoking and everyone else would giggle and munch and RELAX, and I would immediately panic. My eyes would dart frantically around the room, and I'd begin peeking behind the door every forty seconds, certain that the police or my parents were on their way. Everyone would laugh and say, "What is WRONG with you?" and I would cry because everyone was laughing at me and I didn't know why.

My purpose in bingeing, drinking, and drugging was to stop

thinking, and smoking made me think hard and crazy. Also, being stoned with other people is excruciating for a naturally paranoid, high-self-monitor like me. It has always been important to me to act right. I'm a people pleaser, a dancing monkey, always concerned with how *everyone is feeling about me.* But when I was stoned, I couldn't remember how to act. I think that might be the point of being high—to stop acting and just enjoy yourself already—but this was an impossibility for me. I was completely paranoid about *what I should do* versus what I was *actually doing.* I made my friends pay close attention to me and offer frequent updates while I was high.

Pull your earlobe if I'm talking too loud. Check every ten minutes to make sure I haven't peed my pants. Should I say hi to that person? What would I do normally? Would I stand up? Shake her hand? Hug her? Stay seated? Do I like that person? Does she like me? These pretzels are making me thirsty!

Pot did not fill the hole. It stretched it even wider, made me more insecure than ever. It was time to move on to hallucinogens. Enter magic mushrooms.

If pot made me paranoid, shrooms made me completely insane. One night I stayed home, shrooming by myself, and I spent the entire evening conversing with Carmen Electra. She jumped right out of the poster on my boyfriend's wall and sat down in her hot pants to keep me company in my hot pants. We were both concerned about our life choices and confident about our fashion choices, so we found some real camaraderie. Nice girl, that Carmen. And although I really loved and appreciated her that night, it was clear (the next day) that she was not God.

Then one day, like an evil prince on a white horse, cocaine trotted into my nonlife. Cocaine was the one I'd been waiting for. Cocaine was a *Dream.* Cocaine came damn close to filling me up. For a few hours, it erased my insecurities. It made me funny and energized and fabulous and charming, and like I was in on a secret. When cocaine was available, which was always, ten or twelve of us would gather in the back room at a party and do lines all night. The party would rage on outside the door, but we wouldn't leave that room until all the cocaine was gone. Then a friend and I would sneak away to his room, crush his prescription ADD pills, and snort them. I have no idea what effect this had besides helping us concentrate on how wasted and wired and incredibly stupid we were.

I'd do anything to stay UP, because when I came down, I'd remember my hole, and it'd be bigger than ever. But no matter how frantically I'd fill myself with whatever was available—booze, drugs, boys—the sunrise would come. I hated the goddamn sunrise. The sunrise was God stopping by every morning to shine light on my life, and light was the last thing I wanted. So I'd close every blind and try to sleep through daybreak. I'd lie down, heart racing from all the speed, bed spinning from all the booze, and I'd stare at the ceiling and think. I'd think of my parents getting up to go to work to pay for the classes I wasn't taking. I'd think of my friendships that were falling apart. I'd think about Sister, to whom I wouldn't even speak, since I couldn't answer her simple question: *How are you doing?* I'd think about how I had no money, no plans for the future, a deteriorating body, mind, and soul. My brain would torture me for hours, while that sun rose, while the rest of the world started their day. *Their day.* I had no day. I only had night. Those were the worst moments of my life—those sunrises in my college boyfriend's bed.

During one of those sunrises, I sat on the couch alone and looked around the filthy, dark room. I was living there with him because all of my friends had graduated and gone on to careers and life. They were leading their light-filled lives, and I was still in a dark basement. I thought seriously about killing myself that morning. Suicidal thoughts are a neon flashing sign that you're using the *wrong hole filler*.

I like to compare God's love to the sunrise. That sun shows up every morning, no matter how bad you've been the night before. It shines without judgment. It never withholds. It warms the sinners, the saints, the druggies, the cheerleaders—the saved and the heathens alike. You can hide from the sun, but it won't take that personally. It'll never, ever punish you for hiding. You can stay in the dark for years or decades, and when you finally step outside, it'll be there. It was there the whole time, shining and shining. It'll still be there, steady and bright as ever, just waiting for you to notice, to come out, to be warmed. All those years, I thought of God and light and the sun as judgmental, but they weren't. The sunrise was my daily invitation from God to come back to life.

But I wasn't ready. Not yet. So God and the sun continued their vigils while I continued to scoop food, alcohol, and drugs into myself for nearly a decade. I graduated from college, which makes me simultaneously grateful to and suspicious of my alma mater. I became a teacher. My love for my students filled me up for eight hours a day and I won awards for teaching. I was what they call a "highly functional addict." It's worth repeating that sometimes people who need help look nothing like people who need help. Outside of school, I continued to self-destruct. I maxed out my credit cards trying to fill myself up at the mall. I confused sex with love and wound up pregnant. I found myself home alone, after a bewildering day at an abortion clinic. The hole just kept getting bigger, and I was disappearing inside it. I met Craig, but after a few months, I started wondering if we

were taking each other down. We were both drinking and drugging constantly.

Then one day, several months into our relationship, I woke up
sick as a dog. It was Mother's Day, 2002, and I was twenty-five
years old. Once again, I stumbled to the drugstore and bought a
pregnancy test, came home, and peed on the stick. I stared down
at my shaking hands for three long minutes and thought: *Nothing*. I thought nothing.

I looked down at the test and saw that it was positive. Positive.
I was pregnant. I was a hopeless bulimic, alcoholic, drug addict
who was about to become a mother. And I prayed something. I
don't know what. I just prayed, there on the floor. *Help me. Oh
God, help me.*

You see, the hole had gotten bigger and bigger until God fit right
in. He just stepped right in.

When you're all hole, God fits.

That afternoon I quit smoking, drugging, drinking, and bingeing.

I woke up. I married Craig. I had a baby, then another, then a
third. I became a preschool teacher. I became a writer. I became
a good Sister and daughter and friend. Without all the bingeing
and purging, I settled at my natural weight and started to feel
beautiful. So much wasted time and tooth enamel. I became a
person of serious faith. Wavering, doubtful, confused faith, but
faith nonetheless.

I still have a God-sized hole.

I fill it with less poisonous things now, but things that are
equally ineffective. I shop too much. Bubba calls this my "bulimic
shopping." I get antsy and uncomfortable, and instead of sitting
with this feeling, asking what it means, and using it to grow, I

head to the mall and enjoy the adrenaline rush of a shopping binge. Then I feel guilty, so I head back to the mall to purge and return. At the end of the day, I just feel tired and frustrated from using a whole lot of energy to gain zero lasting satisfaction.

I also move a lot. I start feeling empty and restless, and instead of remembering that sometimes life is uncomfortable and empty everywhere, I decide that bliss is just a new house or town or state away. It isn't. Wherever you go, there you are. Your emptiness goes with you. Maddening.

Shopping and moving don't help, but I've discovered a few things that do: writing, reading, water, walks, forgiving myself every other minute, practicing *easy* yoga, taking deep breaths, and petting my dogs. These things don't fill me completely, but they remind me that it is not my job to fill myself. It's just my job to notice my emptiness and find graceful ways to live as a broken, unfilled human—and maybe to help myself and others feel a teeny bit better. Some people of faith swear that their God-shaped hole was filled when they found God, or Jesus, or meditation, or whatever else. I believe them, but that's not been my experience. My experience has been that even with God, life is hard. It's hard just because it's hard being holey.

We have to live with that.

If there's a silver lining to the hole, here it is: the unfillable, God-sized hole is what brings people together. I've never made a friend by bragging about my strengths, but I've made countless by sharing my weakness, my emptiness, and my life-as-a-wild-goose-chase-to-find-the-unfindable.

Holes are good for making friends, and friends are the best fillers I've found yet. Maybe because other people are the closest we get to God on this side. So when we use them to find God in each other, we become holy.

On Writing and Dancing

A friend recently told me that she'd love to write but doesn't because she's not any good at it. I have some thoughts about that.

When I got sober, I dreaded weddings. I was so terrified of weddings that I cried upon receiving invitations. At the weddings I had to attend, I sat straight up in my chair and fake-smiled at the dancing people and prayed that no one would invite me to the dance floor. I tried to look very busy chewing my gum or reapplying lip gloss, and I made many, many unnecessary trips to the ladies' room. The dance floor, sober, was a terrifying place to be avoided at all costs.

During my festive days, I was the first and last one on the dance floor. Thirteen glasses of chardonnay doesn't make a girl confident and sexy, but it sure makes a girl *think* she's confident and sexy. Sober, though, I was too self-conscious to dance. Dancing at a wedding is like being naked out there in plain sight. It's like a *confidence* test. And people dance in groups, so it's also a *belonging* test. It's also, let's face it, a *dancing* test. I have never been an expert at feeling secure, belonging, or dancing. Also, watching other couples lose their inhibitions and just let go with each other made me feel sorry for myself and Craig. I felt like we were missing something important as a couple—like we couldn't really experience fun together. It all made me feel loserish and claustrophobic in my own skin.

At my cousin Natalia's wedding a few years ago, I sat alone at my table, smiling at the couples flirting and pulling each other onto the dance floor. I felt sad for myself. I thought about how much I missed drinking. Then I made myself think a little harder. And it became clear what I was missing wasn't really the drinking, it was the dancing, and nobody was keeping me from dancing. So I stood up and joined Sister and Husband and all of my cousins on the dance floor.

That night, I danced like I'd never danced before. Wildly, horribly, embarrassingly, relentlessly. Sister and Husband understood this to be the breakthrough spiritual experience that it was, so they stayed close, which was helpful. I danced for three hours straight. My hair became a rat's nest, I got sweat stains all over my dress, and I almost broke my ankles twice because I refused to take off my stilettos. Despite Sister's efforts, there were still many of those terrifying moments in which I found myself alone because the dancing circles had closed without me. So I had to awkwardly push my way back into a circle or just close my eyes and sway as if I was so lost in the music that I didn't care that I was alone. Like I *wanted* to be alone, anyway, because I was having a *moment*. Sometimes we have to do that. But I kept dancing, as a gift to myself.

I didn't dance because I was good at it; I did it because I wanted to. Because nobody else can dance for me, no matter how "good" she is. If I feel a yearning to dance, then I'm going to dance. It's not about whether I'm good or secure or I belong. Here's my hunch: nobody's secure, and nobody feels like she completely belongs. Those insecurities are just job hazards of being human. But some people dance anyway, and those people have more fun. On my deathbed, I'm not going to wish I had danced like JLo; I'm just going to wish I had danced more.

The night I first danced sober was one of the most important nights of my life. "Dancing sober" is what I try to do every day. Dancing sober is what I do when I write. I just try to be myself—messy, clumsy, crutchless. *Dancing sober* is just honest, passionate living.

If, anywhere in your soul, you feel the desire to write, please write. Write as a gift to yourself and others. Everyone has a story to tell. Writing is not about creating tidy paragraphs that sound lovely or choosing the "right" words. It's just about noticing who you are and noticing life and sharing what you notice. When you write your truth, it is a love offering to the world because it helps us feel braver and less alone. And if you're a really, really bad writer, then it might be *most* important for you to write because your writing might free other really, really bad writers to have a go at it anyway. Kind of like how watching Sister's confusing lurching on the dance floor finally got me out of my seat at my cousin's wedding. Because I thought, *Well, if she's allowed to keep dancing, certainly no one's going to call me out.*

If you feel something calling you to dance or write or paint or sing, please refuse to worry about whether you're good enough. Just do it. Be generous. Offer a gift to the world that *no one* else can offer: *yourself.*

Day One

To My Friend, on Her First Sober Morning,

I have been where you are. I've lived through this day. This day when you wake up terrified. When you open your eyes and it hits you: *the jig is up*. You lie paralyzed in bed and shake from the horrifying realization that *life as you know it* is over. Then you think that's probably okay, since *life as you know it totally blows*. Even so, you can't get out of bed because the thing is *you don't know how*. You don't know how to live, how to interact, how to cope, how to function without a drink or at least the hope of a future drink. You never learned. You dropped out before all the lessons. So who will teach you how to live?

Listen to me. You are shaking from withdrawal and fear and panic this morning, so you cannot see clearly. You think that this is the worst day of your life, but you are wrong. *This is the best day of your life, friend.* Things, right now, are very, very good—better than they have ever been. Your angels are dancing. Because you have been offered freedom from the prison of secrets. You have been offered the *gift of crisis*.

As Kathleen Norris reminds us, the Greek root of the word *crisis* is "to sift," as in to shake out the excesses and leave only what's important. That's what crises do. They shake things up until we are forced to hold on to only what matters most. The rest falls away. And what matters most right now is that you are sober, so you will not worry about whether the real you will be brave or smart or funny or beautiful or responsible enough. Because the only thing you have to be is sober. You owe the world *absolutely nothing* but sobriety. If you are sober, you are enough. Even if you are shaking and cursing and boring and terrified. You are enough.

But becoming sober, *becoming real,* will be hard and painful. A lot of good things are.

Becoming sober is like recovering from frostbite.

Defrosting is excruciatingly painful. You have been numb for so long. As feeling comes back to your soul, you start to tingle, and it's uncomfortable and strange. But then the tingles start feeling like daggers. Sadness, loss, fear, anger, anxiety—all of these things that you have been numbing with the booze—you feel them for the first time. And it's horrific at first, to tell you the damn truth. But welcoming the pain and refusing to escape from it is the only way to recovery. *You can't go around it, you can't go over it, you have to go through it.* There is no other option, besides amputation. If you allow the defrosting process to take place—if you trust that it will work and choose to endure the pain—one day you will get your soul back. If you can feel, then there has been no amputation. If you can feel, you are not too late.

Friend, we need you. The world has suffered while you've been hiding. You are already forgiven. You are loved. All there is left to do is to step into your life. What does that mean? *What the hell does that mean?*

This is what it means. These are the steps you take. They are plain as mud: Get out of bed. Don't lie there and think—thinking is the kiss of death for us—*just move.* Take a shower. Sing while you're in there. *Make yourself sing.* The stupider you feel, the better. Giggle at yourself, alone. Joy for its own sake—*joy just for you, created by you*—it's the best. Find yourself amusing.

Put on some makeup. Blow-dry your hair. Wear something nice, something that makes you feel grown up. If you have nothing, go buy something. Today's not the day to worry too much about money. Invest in some good coffee, caffeinated and decaf. (Decaf after eleven o'clock.) Read your daughter a story. Don't think about other things while you're reading; actually pay attention to the words. Then braid your girl's hair. Clean the sink. Keep good books within reach. Start with *Traveling Mercies*. David Sedaris is good too. If you don't have any good books, go to the library. If you don't have a library card, apply for one. This will stress you out. You will worry that the librarian will sense that you are a disaster and reject you. Listen: they don't know, and they don't care. They gave me a card, and I've got a rap sheet as long as your arm. When reentering society and risking rejection, the library is a good place to start. They have low expectations. I love the library. Also church. *Both have to take you in.*

As Anne Lamott suggests, only three prayers are necessary. Mine are "Please!" "Thank you!" and "WTF???" That's all the spirituality you'll need for a while. *Go to meetings.* Any meeting will do. Don't worry if the other addicts there are "enough like you." Face it: we are all the same. Be humble.

Get out of the house. If you have nowhere to go, take a walk outside. Do not excuse yourself from walks because it's too cold. Bundle up. The sky will remind you of how big God is, and if you're not down with God, then the oxygen will help. Same thing. Call one friend a day. Do not start the conversation by telling her how *you* are. Ask how *she* is. Really listen to her response, and offer your love. You will discover that you can help a friend just by listening, and this discovery will remind you that you are powerful and worthy.

Get a yoga video and a pretty mat. Practice yoga after your daughter goes to bed. The evenings are dangerous times, so have a plan. Yoga is a good plan because it teaches us to breathe and appreciate solitude as a gift. Learn to keep yourself company.

When you start to *feel, do.* When you start to feel scared because you don't have enough money, find someone to offer a little money. When you start to feel like you don't have enough love, find someone to offer love. When you feel unappreciated and unacknowledged, appreciate and acknowledge someone else in a concrete way. When you feel unlucky, order yourself to consider a blessing or two. Then find a tangible way to make today somebody else's lucky day. These strategies help me sidestep wallowing every day.

Don't worry about whether you like doing these things or not. You're going to hate everything for a long while. And the fact is that you don't even *know* what you like or hate yet. *Just do these things regardless of how you feel about doing these things.* Because these little things, done over and over again, eventually add up to a life. A good one.

Friend, I am sober today. *Thank God Almighty,* I'm sober today. I'm *here,* friend. Yesterday my son turned ten, which means that I haven't had a drink for *ten years and eight months.* Lots of beautiful and horrible things have happened to me during the past ten years and eight months, and I have *handled my business* day in and day out without booze. *GOD, I ROCK.*

Today I'm a wife and a mother and a daughter and a friend and a writer and a dreamer and a Sister to one and a "sister" to thousands of readers. I wasn't any of those things when I was a drunk.

And I absolutely love being a recovering alcoholic. I am more proud of the "recovering" badge I wear than any other.

What will you be, friend? What will you be when you become yourself?

> When Jesus saw her lying there and knew that she had been there for a long time, he said to her, "Do you want to be made well? Then pick up your mat, and walk."
>
> —John 5:6–8

Chutes and Ladders

You know that mind-numbing kids' game, Chutes and Ladders?

Not long ago I thought I had landed on a big chute.

I was driving the kids home from school, and my cell phone rang. It was my doctor. She told me that she had found Lyme disease and an indicator of lupus in my blood. Lyme disease: definitely; lupus: maybe.

I was tested because for weeks I'd been feeling exhausted and sore and cranky, which are all symptoms of autoimmune issues, but they are also just symptoms of motherhood, so we weren't too worried. In my writing, I seem to be extra nice, and I am—at the keyboard and outside in the world—but in my house, I tend to *relax*. It's hard to be on your best behavior all the time. So we thought maybe I just needed some more sleep or coffee. Until the doctor called.

I held the phone in one hand and peeled the kids out of the van with the other. I scurried to the front door and passed them off to Craig, pointed to the phone, and mouthed "doctor." He distracted the kids so I could go back outside and pace up and down the driveway while listening to the confusing details. My doctor explained that since we caught the Lyme early, it was likely that I could beat it, but I would need to immediately begin a double-dose of an antibiotic known to make people very sick. Then she referred me to a specialist about the lupus because it was serious and incurable and my bloodwork looked quite suspicious.

Weird, I thought. I tried to pay attention, but the doctor's voice faded in and out while I stared at the ridiculous metal reindeer in our front yard. I started daydreaming about being on *Oprah*—hailed as the quirky writer who singlehandedly discovered cures for her own incurable diseases. I planned what I would wear to the show. Something classy but whimsical. Then the doctor interrupted my outfit planning with some scary details and I started feeling like I was being pushed down that big chute—you know the one: just when you think you've about won the game, it forces you to start from the beginning. I felt powerless and slippery.

But then I went back inside. And here's what happened in the wake of the Lymie, maybe-lupy news:

Craig and I got dressed up and drove into Washington, D.C., for a fancy dinner to benefit the International Justice Mission, the organization Sister worked with in Africa. There I learned more about slavery and human trafficking and the heroes who storm the darkness to help. I stared at my baby sister across the table, because she is one of those heroes. And I kept thinking of the sign that my friend Josie hung on her classroom wall that said, "We can do hard things." And I thought a lot about how beautiful and powerful courage and faith are when they are found together. I thought, maybe I could be courageous and faithful, in my own little way. Then I went home and slept soundly.

At the crack of dawn the next morning, I called Bubba and Tisha to tell them the news, and they immediately started canceling plans so they could come and stay with us. This is exactly what I wanted them to do. I love when my mom and dad visit. One of my many secrets is that although I look like a grown-up

34

(sort of), I am actually still a little girl who needs to be taken care of and brought snacks and blankets. Bubba sent me this message that day:

> Keep your spirits up. Don't waste your time and energy on negative thoughts. They will all be in the rearview mirror in a few short weeks.
> We will get through this together.
> Lots of help coming from Reedville.
> We love you. Dad and Mom

After breaking the news to Bubba and Tisha, the girls and I drove to my friend Leigha's house. Leigha has chronic Lyme disease, which has wreaked havoc on her life, family, and body. When I got to her house, we let our girls run wild while we sat on the couch and talked. I took notes while she told me every bit of information I needed to know about Lyme. She said that it made her feel grateful to be able to use her struggles to help me. I love Leigha, and I've always hated that when she talked to me about her disease and pain, I could sympathize but I couldn't really understand. There was always a distance between us. On this visit, it felt strangely comforting to me that we were now in the same club. It might be a club that no one else would want to join, but it's a special club just the same. A little Lymie club. Leigha and I became more like family that day, which made me feel cozy.

When the girls and I left Leigha's, we went shopping. Before I knew I was Lymie, I had decided not to buy any extra Christmas decorations. We were trying to simplify because we are very deep and unmaterialistic. Also because money was extra tight (but money was really only 100 percent of the reason). This *no-new-*

stuff rule was okay with me, since Christmas isn't about shiny decorations. But after I found out I was Lymie, I decided that Christmas is a LITTLE about shiny decorations, so the girls and I bought a lot of them.

When we got home, I sent the kids down to the basement, begged them to be nice to each other, and e-mailed Christy. Christy and I have known each other for twenty years. She was by my side when I got drunk, sober, married, and Chase. She is like a beautiful, wise, funny security blanket. I e-mailed her and said I was sad because I seemed to have all of these diseases. She was as shocked and scared and annoyed as I needed her to be. After her initial response, which included lots of capital letters and italics and just the right amount of curses, she said that she was going out for the night but she would order some lime margaritas and get Lupy in my honor.

That night I started my meds, which were supposed to make me very sick. These pills are serious. For example, after taking them, you have to stand up for twenty minutes because if you lie down, the pills could get stuck in your throat and burn a hole in your esophagus. Anyway, after standing for twenty straight minutes without sitting or lying down, by far the hardest part of Lyme so far, Craig and I snuggled in bed with his laptop to watch a movie. He asked me how I was feeling every few minutes, which I love. Halfway through the movie I got thirsty, so I said, "I'm not feeling so good," and Craig popped out of bed and literally ran to the kitchen to get me ginger ale. I actually felt fine, just extra warm and cozy and unsure about movement. But I don't think it's necessary to share everything all the time. Besides, being cared for by Craig makes being sick worth it.

Craig let me sleep in the next morning, and when I finally crept out to the family room, there was a fire in the fireplace, blocks and Christmas books everywhere, Christmas music playing, and four Meltons on the floor relaxing in their jammies. I joined them, and after several hours of playing like this, the thought crossed my mind that I should probably go do something productive, like Christmas or grocery shopping. Then I thought, but *How can I POSSIBLY DO ANYTHING? I have LYME, for Pete's sake.* So we stayed in front of the fire in our pajamas and read books and laughed and ate junk food all day. That night we went to Gena's house, where we shared a magical evening of old friends and delicious food and a visit from Santa. We hugged and laughed until we cried, and then we expressed our awe that a group of sorority sisters could turn into a mob of women and husbands and babies and love so quickly. We had helped each other grow up, and now we were watching our children grow up together. Together is so good. Not easy, but good.

Here's what I learned in the wake of my Lyme news: it's really hard to distinguish between a chute and a ladder. The days following my diagnosis were filled with little miracles. Maybe all my days are filled with little miracles, but I'm too distracted by what I think is my life to notice them. Sometimes bad news is the best way to see all the good quickly and clearly. Bad news has a way of waking us up, sort of like a glass of cold water in the face. We might prefer waking in a gentler way, but we can't argue with the efficiency of the cold-water method. And we'll take it if it means we're not going to sleep through the party.

In Case of Emergency

"What is to give light must endure burning."
—Viktor E. Frankl

Sometimes when I call Sister, she answers with, "Well, hello, *In Case of Emergency*," since those words accompany my number on her screen. Long ago we read that it's a good idea to add an "ICE" to your contacts so that if something horrible happens, the person who finds you will know whom to call. So Sister refers to me as "In Case of Emergency" and I call her "Sister." They mean the same thing.

Something horrible did happen to Sister seven years ago. Three years prior, she married a man whom she loved with every inch of her gigantic heart. Well, we thought she loved him with every inch, but we didn't understand the true capacity of her heart back then. We don't believe anymore that anyone loves with her whole heart, just pieces of her broken heart. Now we know that in order for love to be real and true and good, you need to have had your heart shattered. We know now that a broken heart is not the end of the world, but a beginning. Back then, we were still trying to run from broken hearts. We didn't understand yet what Joanna Macy meant when she wrote that "the heart that breaks open can contain the universe."

Sister's heart shattered when, after the torment of a few con-founding, excruciating weeks, her husband decided that he was finished being married to her. Because he was abroad throughout much of their marriage, she learned that it was over via e-mail. Just months earlier, we'd bought homes within a mile of each other, with dreams of raising our babies together. But one after-noon it all fell apart, as it does. I sat on the wood floor below Sister's desk chair, rocking Tish in her infant seat, kissing her forehead and inhaling her new baby smell. While Sister read her e-mail, I held Tish's teeny hand and looked up to see Sister's face darken and fall. Then I watched my best friend crumble out of her chair and melt onto the floor next to Tish and me. She curled up in a ball with her hands covering her head, her back to me, the world, and the sky. She heaved and rocked and moaned. Her posture and the noises she made reminded me of a dying animal. I touched my baby Sister's quivering back, and I looked up at the ceiling and said aloud, "God**DAMNIT**. GodDAMNIT. *GOD-DAMNIT*." It was important to me that God knew immediately that I held him completely responsible for Sister's pain. I pulled out my WTF? billboard prayer and turned it toward the heavens on behalf of Sister.

For months I'd begged God to save her marriage. I'd asked Him to help her, one of his finest creations: a woman who val-ues honor, loyalty, truth, and commitment more than any other person I've ever known. A woman who'd spent every moment of her life doing the right thing. She'd earned straight As from birth. She was both the most popular girl in school and the kind-est. She specialized in including everyone, especially the loners. She labored through a top-notch university, graduated with honors and spent her weekends volunteering in the state's only maximum security women's jail, studying the cycle of domestic violence, and making friends. After her first year of college, she flew to Ireland by herself to learn firsthand about her ancestors and The Troubles. After graduating, she moved to Hawaii for a few months to care for a friend's grandmother, sling pizzas, and learn to surf. From Hawaii she traveled alone to Mexico to build houses for the homeless. Then she came home and suffered through law school to make a difference for the powerless with her big brain and heart and education. All the while, she cared for the largest and smallest needs of our family and friends. She was the role model for everyone who knew her. She was *good*, good enough to deserve a good man. And of all the things she'd gotten right in her life, she believed that marriage was the most important.

I was the prodigal daughter; she was the steadfast one. And there we were. I, with two babies and a husband at home. She, shattered on the floor. I'd never done a productive thing in my life except get sober and make babies. I'd done everything backward. She'd done everything, forever, by the book. The right way. Until then, I'd only learned this about grace: sometimes, like in my case, you get blessed for no reason. You get something wonderful that you don't deserve. But on that day, I learned that the flip side is also true: sometimes you get *screwed* for no reason. You get something awful that you never, ever deserved. It all slips away. You cannot earn yourself an easy life or even a fair one.

Soon after *The Day It All Fell Apart*, Sister moved in with us. This brilliant, beautiful, accomplished woman moved into a teeny, cold room in our basement. She never missed a day of work. Her work was hard—often fifteen hours a day hard. She came home late and cried most nights. I'd sit with her and cry too. She couldn't eat much, but Craig would grill her favorites, and I'd try to convince her to eat a few bites. I'd bring her water in the evening and coffee in the morning. There were no words to offer that didn't ring of Pollyanna hope and absurdity. I had absolutely nothing I could use to take her pain away. She cried herself to sleep in our basement. Sometimes I'd stand outside her bedroom and angrily pray or sit silently with my back against her door. I was holding vigil, making sure that no more sadness entered that room. It was my ridiculous attempt to protect her.

During that year, I was attached to the phone. I was *always* on the phone, listening to Sister cry or try *not* to cry, which was worse. The tortuous days following The Day It All Fell Apart passed slowly. Small bits of information made their way to her and then me, just enough to make each day crueler than the last. The costs incurred by the divorce were equally devastating. Time was relentless and heavy. It felt as if we were going through life with refrigerators strapped to our backs. It was hard to breathe, hard to feel anything but weight and self-pity and anger. After hours on the phone with Sister, giving her nothing but bewildered, agonizing silence and sincere but impotent offerings and platitudes like, *"God, I'm so sorry. I love you so much,"* I'd have to call my parents to give them the daily report: the information about Sister's mental and emotional state on that particular day. I was the go-between. Sister couldn't do it because it was too hard to say twice and because she had a tremendous amount of work to get done and a stiff upper lip to maintain at her law firm. But also because we both knew that my parents were the most heart-broken of all.

My Sister is their Baby, and this was a knock-out blow. My dad was angrier than he'd ever been. He was also incredibly tender with her, but we could all sense the rage below the surface. He is her father, and he considers it his lifelong responsibility and honor to protect his babies from pain. Now, once again, one of his daughters was suffering through something he'd never had to face, walking a path he hadn't blazed before for us, and that seemed all but impossible for him to survive. So Sister felt it was her responsibility to help assuage *his* anger, *his* pain. And she just didn't have the strength to lead anyone else through the darkness.

My mother was equally devastated—so devastated, in fact, that it was hard for her to let it be as awful as it was. She was hopeful. She had to be, because allowing it to really sink in, accepting that there was no way out of the pain that her baby girl was going through, no matter how much "hope" we directed her way, was unfathomable. So she said things that occasionally made Sister feel that she was being pushed through her grief too fast.

I learned that in these disasters, all we can do is tell our In Case of Emergencies that their grief is real, and if it lasts forever, then we will grieve with them forever.

As far as I was able to tell during those two years, there was nothing else worth saying. It was not going to be all right, ever. Everything doesn't happen for a decent reason. I was Sister's In Case of Emergency and I couldn't fix her emergency. I couldn't do anything at all except feed her, hold her when she cried, pray angry prayers, keep showing up, and hope that time and my home and presence would offer healing.

I also learned that the In Case of Emergency needs a whole lot of help too. One day I called my parents and said, "You need to come today. TODAY. I need help. It feels like too much today. I'm going to break if I don't get some air. I need to spend one night not watching her cry. My heart is shattering."

My mom was so worried about me that she said, "Honey, maybe this is too much for your family. You need to be with your husband and children. Maybe we need to make different living arrangements." And I froze. I said, "No. NO. Mom, please come here and help me today. But please, don't ever, ever breathe a word to Sister about how hard this is for me. Not a word, not a glance, nothing, *nothing* that will make her feel like a burden. She is not a burden. She is a gift. Carrying her through this is an honor—it's the most important thing I've ever done in my life. I just need some help. Come today, and then go and let me get back to work."

She did. She always does. My parents ALWAYS show up.

Time passed slowly. I would not say we made progress. Everything went in circles, cycles. One afternoon there would be laughter, but it would fall apart again by evening. Time was not a forward march toward hope. It was just a waiting time, like we were all in a bunker together waiting out some nuclear fallout and wondering when, if ever, it'd be safe to go outside again.

What's funny is that I remember this as one of the hardest things my little family has ever endured. My children and Craig had little to none of my attention. My heart and mind were always on Sister. But when I asked Craig what he remembered about that time, he said, "That was fun, wasn't it? Having her with us?" That's all he remembers, really. Just enjoying her company. No wonder she healed at my house.

Sister started dating again after a year. It was horrible. She described dating after the divorce as getting vicious food poisoning from a cheeseburger and then being forced to eat burger after burger while you're still nauseated by the first one. Sister is beautiful and smart and hilarious, and it seemed that each man she dated would fall in love with her, and then she'd have to break his heart, which would break hers wide open again. Each breakup tossed her right back into her original pain. It was like ripping a bandage off an open wound again and again and again.

Eventually the day came for her to move out. I was terrified and dead set against it. I did not think she was ready. But she reminded me that I would never think she was ready, because *I* was not ready. I did not trust the world with her anymore. But she went out into the world anyway. The day she moved out, she'd been dating a boy. Everyone knew he wasn't THE boy, but he was a good and kind one. He was the one to hold her hand while she walked toward the moving van sitting in front of my house. He was there to share the physical and emotional burden of moving out and on. I'll never forget watching the two of them walking away, hand in hand. I've done this only three times in my life, but after I closed the door behind her, I fell to my knees on the floor. I started speaking to God kindly again, for the first time in a year. I said, *Thank you,* there seems to be hope. *Thank you,* because she's still walking. *Thank you,* for sending a strong, good man to help her take this next step. Life is so, so incredibly burdensome—much more so without a partner to share the weight.

Sister moved in with friends. She broke up with the Good-But-Not-the-One Boy. Life continued to be hard. More confusing information came in about her ex-husband. Her friends started buying homes and having babies.

One day my friend Joanna called me to ask my permission to set up Sister with our mutual friend, John. I was scared and said, "No, no, nope. Absolutely not." Joanna kept asking. Three months later, I said, "Fine." He asked for a picture. I sent one of Sister and Tish holding hands crossing a busy street. John replied that he felt like Sister might be too young for him, but the crossing guard was a stunner. I laughed, but just a little.

They had their first date at an Irish pub. John told me later that when Sister walked in, he fell speechless for the first time in his life. He stumbled through hellos. She ordered a Guinness. He thought he'd died and gone to Irish Boy heaven.

They stayed at their table for hours and got kicked out when the pub closed. He walked her to her car, and they both got in and talked into the wee hours of the early morning, when the street sweeper made them leave. I remember getting Sister's call later that day and hearing something in her voice that made me think *Oh. God. He's gonna be the One.*

I KNEW it. He was. Soon everyone knew it.

But Sister wasn't ready to know it. She had work to do. Although we did everything in our power to stop her, she took a year-long leave from her law firm and applied to work for the International Justice Mission.

Sister was sent to Rwanda. She was to be there for a year. She and John had been dating for six months when she decided to go, but he supported her fully. He said, "Go. Go do what you need to do. I will be here waiting for you."

We all said that. It was a very, very hard thing to say.

Sister spent the year finding and saving child rape victims and prosecuting child rapists. Occasionally she'd call and explain to me over a horrible connection that she'd been searching through huts to reunite a baby with its family, or that she was at an orphanage holding sick children. I'd say, "Listen. I don't want to hear it. I spent two hours at *freaking Chuck E Cheese today.*"

"You win!" Sister would say.

My parents spent the year in terror—terror mixed with ferocious pride. Sister started telling me on the phone that she was considering the possibility that she wasn't meant to marry. Perhaps God was calling her to lead a life of adventure and service. That maybe she should stay in Africa to continue saving children from evil.

I supported this noble idea *not at all*. I told her that I thought she was afraid of committing again. I told her that perhaps it felt safer to spend her life saving humanity than to risk loving one human being again. We talked about how loving one person hard and long and well is the hardest thing on earth to do.

She came home. She came home to us—to John, really. Soon after, John asked for my sister's hand in marriage. My dad said the following: *If you hurt her, you are going to need to find a country far, far away where I will not be able to find you. Because I will try. I will spend the rest of my life trying to find you.*

"I am not going to hurt her," John said. John is a good, honest man, and we all knew he was The One for Sister. But we were still scared to death. None of us was sure, after walking through the pain, that it was better to have loved and lost than never to have loved at all. When Sister accepted John's proposal, I gave her a necklace that said, "I am not afraid. I was born to do this," a quote attributed to Joan of Arc before she charged into battle. I knew that for Sister, entering marriage again took every bit of her courage.

On their wedding day, I gave a toast in which I explained that as Sister's In Case of Emergency, I know what a responsibility it is to be the best friend and caretaker of such a masterpiece of a human being. To John, my parents, Craig, our friends and family, and to Sister, I said:

Sister. She's a masterpiece. People feel it when they first meet her. They sense it even when they walk by her. Last week we were out shopping and three different middle-aged men stopped us on the sidewalk and said, "I'm sorry, but I just have to tell you how beautiful you are." She smiled and thanked them graciously but without a hint of surprise, because it happens to her all the time.

But there are beautiful people, and then there is beauty like my Sister's. Beauty that comes from being born with unshakable, superhuman integrity. Beauty that comes from intelligence matched with wisdom. Beauty that is compassion combined with courage. The beauty that comes from being a woman who can be trusted. All who are lucky enough to know her know this beauty. We know that she's a work of art. But not everyone knows the process the artist used to create her.

I do. My whole life has been about paying attention to my Sister. Everything she has ever learned or feared or dreamed or wondered has been important to me, and so I've memorized it all. I know what she wore every single first day of school since kindergarten. I know she still has most of those outfits. I remember the entire speech she gave when she ran for president of her elementary school, and I remember word-for-word the commencement speech she delivered at her high school graduation. I know the name of her first Cabbage Patch Kid and the names of our, I mean her, future children. I know what she's thinking right now and exactly what her facial expression will be when this toast is done and the colors she'll paint her first house. I am my Sister's biography. I am the song that should be written about her and the poem and the play and the prayer. I've got it all, right here. Recording it all, bearing witness to such an amazing life, has been the honor of my life.

Being Sister's sister is like being a museum curator charged with both protecting and displaying a priceless piece of art. When someone comes close to look, I have to make sure he gets it. I have to make sure he's paying enough attention. I have to make sure that he understands the value of the artwork. I have to make sure he's approaching with the right mix of curiosity and reverence. I have to make sure he's in the proper state of AWE.

But when I explained all of this to Craig, he told me that those

museum people, the ones who tell you all the things about the art?
They're annoying.

And he said, "John gets it. He gets her. He knows. He soaks her
in. He is in awe."

"I know," I said.

Enjoy your masterpiece, John. You deserve her. I know, from
experience, that with her in it, your life will be filled with joy and
magic. And a lot of shoes.

If you are blessed enough to be someone's In Case of Emergency
and you are called upon, keep being who you have always been.
Do what you've always done. There is a reason your friend chose
you for that role, so don't freeze. Keep moving. Trust your instincts.

Go to her. Don't call first, because she won't know she wants
you there until you arrive and sit down. Don't ask, "What can I
do?" She doesn't know. Just do *something*. When you go to her
house, bring a movie in case she doesn't want to talk. If she does
want to talk, avoid saying things to diminish or explain away her
pain, like, "Everything happens for a reason," or "Time heals all
wounds," or "God gives us only what we can handle." These are
things people say when they don't know what else to say, and
even if they're true, they're better left unsaid because they can be
discovered only in retrospect. When her pain is fresh and new, let
her have it. Don't try to take it away. Forgive yourself for not having that power. Grief and pain are like joy and peace; they are not
things we should try to snatch from each other. They're sacred.
They are part of each person's journey. All we can do is offer relief
from this fear: *I am all alone.* That's the one fear you can alleviate.
Offer your In Case of Emergency your presence, your love, yourself, so she'll understand that no matter how dark it gets, she's
not walking alone. That is **always** enough to offer, Thank God.

Grief is not something to be fixed. It's something to be borne, together. And when the time is right, there is always something that is born *from* it. After real grief, we are reborn as people with wider and deeper vision and greater compassion for the pain of others. We know that. So through our friend's grief, we maintain in our hearts the hope that in the end, good will come of it. But we don't say that to our friend. We let our friend discover that on her own. Hope is a door each one must open for herself.

Today, Sister and I are both brokenhearted in all the best ways. She helped heal me, I helped heal her, and we heal each other all over again, every single day. We are honored to be wounded healers. Good has come of it all.

Sister and John just welcomed their first child into this beautiful world.

Love wins.

Inhale, Exhale

Reading is my *inhale* and writing is my *exhale*. If I am not reading and writing regularly, I begin to suffocate and tend to climb the nearest person like a frantic cat, clawing at the person's eyeballs and perching on his head, desperate to find a breath of air. This is why my husband is supportive of my writing, because he is generally the nearest person. So Craig and I think it's imperative for a girl to have a place to inhale and exhale. Some place safe to tell the truth.

We're not often permitted to tell the truth in everyday life. There is a small set of words and reactions and pleasantries we are allowed to say, like, "I'm fine, and you?" But we are not supposed to say much of anything else, especially how we are really doing. We find out early that telling the whole truth makes people uncomfortable and is certainly not ladylike or likely to make us popular, so we learn to lie sweetly so that we can be loved. And when we figure out this system, we are split in two: the public self, who says the right things in order to belong, and the secret self, who thinks other things.

At one point I got so sick of listening to my self drone on to other women about little league and countertops and how fine I was, that I decided to kill my public self. The truth is that I am very rarely fine. I am usually so far behind fine that I couldn't find fine with binoculars. Or so far past fine that I expect the birds to notice my superhuman joy and start speaking to me. Based on the successful Tess experiment, I told Craig I was going to start introducing my secret self to other moms at the playground and the mall. The introduction would sound something like this:

"Hi, I'm Glennon. I'm a recovering, well, everything, and most recently I've been struggling with isolation and intimacy with my husband and I've also been getting quite angry with my kids for no reason. I feel awful about these things. But yoga is helping. Also deep breaths and baths. How are you?"

If she answered honestly, great—new friend! And if she ran away, great too! At least we'd know right away that we didn't match. I thought it was a brilliant, efficient plan.

But Sister said, "Please, honey, promise me you won't do that. For the sake of your kids and the community." She went on to explain that these types of things are not appropriate to share at the playground even if they're true. Strangers trying to help their kids across the monkey bars don't necessarily want to hear about my anxiety and ecstasy and confusion. She said that sometimes it's right to filter what we are really thinking to protect ourselves and family from utter humiliation and just to keep society running smoothly. I asked her if "filter" meant "lie," and she said yes, definitely.

Of course, Sister was right. I understand. But I still think it's vital for a girl to share her truthful, secret self somewhere. In order to avoid going a little batty, she must have a place to say the things she is actually thinking when she is either saying *appropriate* things or saying nothing at all due to the filter/lying policy.

So it goes for a child, too, because the split between the secret self and the public self happens early and hard. Every little girl is told at some point that the world does not want to see the ugly, afraid, secret version of her. Sometimes the people who tell her this are advertisers, sometimes they're people close to her, and sometimes they're just her own demons.

And so she must be told by someone she trusts that this hiding is both necessary and unnecessary.

She must be taught that, in fact, some people *will* want and need to hear about her secret self as badly as they need to inhale. Because reading her truth will make them less afraid of their own secret selves. And she must be taught that telling her truth will make her less afraid too. Because maybe her secret self is actually her own personal prophet.

She also must be warned that her truth will undoubtedly make some people uneasy and angry, so she'll need to share it strategically, perhaps through art, which God offers as a safe way to express joy and madness. And she'll need a trusted person to help her find her medium, so she won't feel that she has to hide or hold her breath any longer. Because when she exhales, she'll discover that she's created the space to inhale again, and that will keep her going.

And this, the importance of *this lesson,* is why I became a teacher.

Now I didn't tell all of this to my students, because many were only three years old.

But sometimes, when I could see that one of my students was feeling really angry or left out, I would call her over to the writing table and write the words MAD or LEFT OUT in big red letters and read it to her with gusto. Sometimes I added lightning bolts and a frowny face. And occasionally her eyes would light up because she'd figured out that I have a mad, left-out secret self too—that it feels like lightning and frowns just like hers—and she would smile.

Usually, though, she'd look perplexed and start talking about how her dog peed on the family room carpet the night before. And I'd say, "Awesome. Wanna write about it?"

Smelly Coughy Guy

Here's why I really love and need yoga: because of Smelly Coughy Guy.

I am easily overwhelmed. There are lots of things I have to do each day to remind myself that everyone is okay, including me. Yoga is one of these things I do to stay calm and remember. Yoga is like a sabbath; it's how I prove to myself that I am not in charge, that if I drop off the face of the earth for an hour with no other goal than to breathe, the world will keep spinning without me. Because, as it turns out, I am not the one causing it to spin. I'm just along for the ride. I practice yoga to find quiet and peace and stillness: to prove to myself that those things exist. I also practice yoga to learn how not to be bothered by things that are out of my control. That's how I want to be. And people have to practice if they ever hope to be how they want to be.

I practice yoga at my local gym. When I am not writing or frantically searching for sippy cups, I am at the gym. Not because I am really all that interested in fitness, but because my gym has a wonderful nursery full of people who will take my kids, so I "work out" a lot. If my post office had a wonderful nursery full of people who would take my kids, I would mail a lot. Sometimes Adrianne and I meet at the gym and just sit on the stationary bikes and talk. We don't even move our legs. After Adrianne and

I finish not working out, I go to yoga. She doesn't go because she thinks yoga's stupid.

So I say bye to Adrianne, and I walk into the dark, quiet yoga room. I get my mat and set it up way over in the corner. I make a border with my water bottle and shoes as a subtle hint that nobody should get too close to me. I smile at my instructor and get into the lotus position and close my eyes and start breathing deeply through my nose. Aaaaaah . . .

And then . . . Smelly Coughy Guy walks in the door. I know it's him right away because I hear him and I smell him. Smelly Coughy Guy smells and coughs. That's all he does. And so every time he walks into class, I panic and I pray silently and ferociously: *pleasenopleasenopleasenodontsitnexttomedontsitnextome.* And *every single time,* he sets up his mat right next to mine. Every single time. Sometimes he even *moves my water bottle* to get closer to me. And he smells and he coughs throughout the entire class. He smells and he coughs so insistently and consistently that when the instructor says to breathe deeply, I'm not sure that's in my best interest.

I spend the first half-hour of class silently cursing Smelly Coughy Guy. I fold my hands in prayer pose and bow my little head and half-close my eyes, and then I ignore my instructor's pleas to focus and stay in the moment, and I glare sideways at Smelly Coughy Guy every time he coughs. I often get caught by my instructor, who smiles zenly at both of us. And that makes me share my glare with her. And I keep saying to my poor beleaguered self, *Why me? Why why why? I'm with three screaming kids at home all day. Is it too much to ask for just an hour of peace and quiet?*

I do this every time. Still.

But here's what I'm learning from Smelly Coughy Guy and

my patient, nonjudgmental yoga instructor: *I think I may have had the wrong idea about what peace is.*

I pray and pray for God to help me feel some peace and stillness in the midst of my mommy life instead of feeling constantly like a dormant volcano likely to erupt at any given moment and burn my entire family alive. And God says: *Well G, here's the thing. Peace isn't the absence of distraction or annoyance or pain. It's finding Me, finding peace and calm,* **in the midst** *of those distractions and annoyances and pains.*

So he sends me Smelly Coughy Guy, a kind teacher, and an otherwise quiet room to practice finding peace.

Smelly Coughy Guy is actually part of the answer to my prayers. He's helping me.

I am learning a little more each day.

For example, last weekend my family was running late for a birthday party, and when we finally got everybody's shoes on and the whole family strapped into the van, gifts and sippy cups in sticky little hands, the garage door wouldn't open. We were just sitting in the van, kids yelling because they were afraid we'd miss the party, hands freezing, for a solid ten minutes, and Craig couldn't fix the door. It was not good.

But I didn't even burst out crying. I said to myself, "Self, this too, shall pass."

And this, my friends, was progress. Or maybe it was the fumes. Either way, Craig called it a "miracle."

> Peace is not the absence of conflict, but the ability to cope with it.
>
> —Robert Fulghum

COMMITTING

Birthdays

Let's head back to the morning of March 20, 2003, for a moment, shall we?

Craig and I have been married for six months. Chase, our first-born, is two months old. Skip the math and stay with me. I'm home on maternity leave and spend my days alternating between the ecstasy and despair that accompany caring for an infant. I'm a little worn out.

But on March 20, I wake up renewed, refreshed, and tingling with excitement because as soon as I open my eyes, I remember: it's my birthday. *MY BIRTHDAY!* I lie in bed and wait for the surprises and festivities and *celebration of me* to begin.

I wait. Then I wait a little longer. I look at Craig sleeping soundly and think, *Ooooh—this is gonna be good.* He's still asleep! He must've been up all night preparing for my big day. Can't wait.

Still waiting. Staring at Craig.

Craig opens his eyes, turns to me, and smiles. *Happy birthday, honey.* I bat my eyes and smile back.

Craig gets up and stumbles to the shower.

I stay in bed. Still waiting. Waiting patiently.

He comes back twenty minutes later and says, "Can I make you some coffee?"

Um. *Yeah.*

I climb out of bed. I put my hair up and throw on some makeup so I'll look nice in the pictures Craig's sure to snap of me when I emerge from the bedroom and see all my balloons and flowers and perhaps the string quartet he's hired to play while I eat the fancy breakfast he's prepared.

I take a deep breath and fling open the bedroom door with much birthday gusto. I prepare my most surprised face.

Turns out there was no need to prepare. I *am* surprised. Because there are no balloons. No quartet. No *nothing*. Just Craig. Smiling, hugging me. *"Happy Birthday, honey. Gotta go. See you for dinner tonight?"*

Craig leaves. I sit on the kitchen floor of our teeny apartment wondering if this is a practical joke. I repeatedly open and close the front door in case he's hiding there with all of my friends whom he's flown in from the ends of the earth to yell "SURPRISE!" at me. No friends. Nothing.

I sit on the couch, shocked. I am misunderstood. I am unappreciated.

Growing up, birthdays were a big deal. Bubba and Tisha made the world stop on my birthday. I never knew what would happen, but I knew it was going to be good. Tisha served breakfast in bed with flowers and gifts, and out-of-the-ordinary things happened all day. In high school, Bubba sent roses to my fourth-period history class with a card that said, "From your secret admirer." *Nobody* was allowed to get flowers delivered to class, but Bubba *knew* people. He also knew that those flowers would make me the most popular girl in school for the day, and they did. I walked around shrugging my shoulders when people asked me who they were from, glancing nonchalantly in the direction of the captain of the football team, who didn't know my name. *Anything was possible* on my birthday.

Let's just say that the morning of March 20, 2003, I did not feel like the most popular girl in school. I did not feel like *anything could happen*. I felt like *nothing* could happen. Deflated, I sat down on the couch with my crying baby and turned on the TV. The news anchor announced that America had officially declared some sort of war. *What???* I yelled at the TV. *On my birthday?????*

That was IT.

I called Craig at work. He didn't answer, so I hung up and called back immediately, which is our bat signal for *it's an emergency*. He answered on the first ring, "Hi, What's wrong? Is everything okay? Another fire???"

I had set the apartment on fire the previous week. Twice. Firefighters had come both times. Blaring their sirens and holding their big hoses and wearing their big masks and costumes and everything, which I thought was a little dramatic of them. The fires weren't *that* big. But Craig was still a little jumpy. Anyway, that's not the point of this story. For the love of God, try to focus on *MY BIRTHDAY*.

Me: No, husband. There is no fire. It is much worse than that. You should know that I have cancelled my birthday. Today is no longer my birthday.

Craig: What? Why?

Me: Because it is early afternoon and nothing extraordinary has happened to me yet. Except, apparently, some sort of war. I hate this day. And so it is not my birthday. Cancel it in your brain. Tomorrow is my birthday.

Craig: Okay. Ooooookay. Should I cancel our reservations and the sitter for tonight?

Me: No. No you shouldn't, Honey. We will still go out to dinner tonight. But it will be a working dinner. Bring a pencil and paper, because tonight I will hold a seminar just for you about my *birthday expectations*. They are many and they are specific, so you will want to wear your thinking cap. Also, find a sitter and make reservations for tomorrow night too. *Tomorrow night* will be my birthday dinner. My birthday is *tomorrow*. Consider it a second chance. You are welcome. See you tonight, Love. For the seminar.

We went to dinner that night, and I explained to Craig that my parents showed their love by *celebrating* special days. I told him that they paid attention to what I really wanted and cared about, offered thoughtful gifts, and created meaningful traditions. I explained that this is how I learned to accept love. So when he didn't do that, it made me feel panicked and unloved somewhere down really deep.

Craig explained that he loved me very much. And because he loved me, he wanted me to *feel* loved. But he said that it's hard to know what makes a person feel loved best. So he thought it was kind and wise that I figured out what made me feel loved and shared it with him. He said he was grateful. It made him feel safe, like I would help him through this marriage thing instead of being secretly resentful.

The Love Seminar worked for us. There was crying, laughing, and lots of talking about how hard it is to come from two different families and make a new one. We talked about how impossible it is to read minds and hearts and what a relief it is to hear what the person you love needs and learn how to give it. To set each other up for success rather than failure.

The next morning, on March 21, 2003, *my temporary birthday*, Craig walked into our bedroom with hot coffee and bagels covered with pink candles. He sang to me and asked me to make a wish.

When I peeked out of the bedroom I saw posters covering the walls of our apartment. They said, HAPPY BIRTHDAY, HONEY! I LOVE MY AMAZING WIFE! The posters had balloons and hearts drawn all over them. Boys can't really draw balloons and hearts. Ridiculously cute.

I squealed and Craig beamed. I kissed him good-bye and he said he'd call soon. Every hour, in fact.

I peeked into Chase's room and saw that his crib was decorated with blue streamers.

I went to pee, unrolled some toilet paper, and little sticky notes fell out of the roll, "Happy birthday baby!"

Teamwork. Love takes teamwork, I think.

These days, Craig is known for his skill at celebrating special family days. He takes pride in it. He is a *master*. Legendary. I can't tell you how many times a friend has said to me, "You are so *lucky*. He is amazing."

And part of me wants to say, "*Lucky?* Whadyathink? He fell out of the sky like that?"

But instead I say, "I know. He is."

Lucky Seven

Dear Craig,

One night, not all that long ago, after we put the kids to bed, you and I squeezed alongside each other on our big green couch and stared at the pictures of our babies on the mantle. We noticed together how lovable and perfect they were frozen in those pictures, unable to move or pinch each other or beg for dessert. We discussed how achingly much we loved them, especially when they were asleep. After some quiet, I said, "I love you more today than I did on our wedding day." A moment passed before you replied, "Me too. But to be fair, we didn't really love each other that much on our wedding day."

My eyes widened and I sat up quickly and tried to decide if my feelings were hurt. Then we burst out laughing, and I cried a little. It was the first time we'd acknowledged how confusing and terrifying that day was. That day in your parents' backyard when we met at the end of a long white aisle and promised to love each other 'til death, certain only that we had two things in common: the little one inside me, and the shared belief that eventually, if we just did the *next right thing* as we understood it, Everything Would Be Okay.

It was the first time we'd admitted to each other that ours was a type of arranged marriage, like they have in India. Only instead of by tradition and parents, ours was arranged by too much wine and too few precautions. And God, maybe. But did I love you that day? I guess I couldn't have, because I didn't even know you then. You were a gift I hadn't yet unwrapped.

I didn't know that when we brought Chase home from the hospital and laid him on the floor of our little apartment, I would look at your face and see that there was *nothing more to worry about*, because it was clear that you were officially hooked on us.

I didn't know that you and I would lie in bed together each night, hold hands under the covers, and ask God to protect our babies and each other. I didn't know that I'd awaken during your midnight newborn shifts and hear you singing to our baby girl. I didn't know that you'd allow Sister to fall into our home and arms and that you'd rebuild her broken heart one hug, one grilled turkey burger, one silly dance at a time.

I didn't know that your goodness, your generosity, and your loyalty would be lifeboats to my parents during the storm of their lives. That all by yourself, just being who you are, you would preserve their faith in people.

I didn't know that you'd hold me tight the nights our adoptions fell through and whisper to me not to worry, because we'd never give up.

I didn't know that when you left each morning, I'd have your gentle spirit in Chase, your playfulness in Tish, and your affection in Amma to keep me company.

And I didn't know when I started recording our silly, seemingly insignificant daily adventures, that what I'd end up with, on second glance, is a Love Story.

Fireworks

I met Craig on July Fourth, 2000, at an all-day bar crawl in Washington, D.C. A bar crawl is an event during which hundreds of people travel together from one bar to the next, drinking heavily at each one. The purpose of the traveling is to make the drunk people feel like they are accomplishing something, in addition to the usual liver and reputation damage. During this event, entire D.C. blocks were closed off from traffic and the streets were packed with guys and girls holding plastic cups and performing for each other.

It was just 10:00 a.m. when I first saw Craig, so I'd had only three or seven beers and I was still lookin' good. I stood on a curb with one of my oldest and best friends, Dana, and we scanned the sea of people together. I saw Craig and thought, *"Hmmmm."* He was tan and laughing. Craig is *always* tan and laughing.

I pinched Dana. She knew him, I remembered that. Craig was a year ahead of Dana and me in high school. Dana grew up next door to him, and she and her friends used to meet at her house to peek out the window and watch Craig mow the lawn shirtless. Dana's mommy, whom I love, told me later that she and *her* friends used to do the exact same thing at bridge club.

So Dana and I walked over to say hi. She introduced us. Craig smiled real big and his eyes squinched up like they do and my stomach did that flip-flop thing. I was petrified. I am petrified of all boys, always have been, always will be. Craig was gorgeous and wearing blue and smiling, and I thought, *I'm going to die.* We talked for a while. I have no idea what we talked about, because I was thinking about looking hot and cool at the same time, and this is really difficult after seven drinks in 95 degree weather. Our conversation ended too soon. My friends found me and his found him. We said bye and smiled at each other. It was way too early and awkward and bright to ask for numbers.

We went our separate ways to attend to the important business of drinking our weight in beer and doing regrettable things.

Then: TWELVE hours later.

It's 10:00 p.m. I'm on the dance floor at the eighth and final bar of the day. I've just finished flailing around with my girls to "I Will Survive." Now I find myself dancing with a boy who tells me he's going to call me the following day so I can go on his boat. I remember thinking two things:

#1. You *so* do not have a boat.
#2. Must think of fake phone number fast. Why can't I remember what a *number* is?

I look over behind the bar and see Craig standing there, ordering a beer. The bartender appears to be flirting with him. I am grateful the bartender is a boy.

I think: *Oh God Oh God Oh God.*

I abandon lying boat man and sneak off the dance floor.

I stand off by myself, drinking my beer, trying to look both available and busy. In case Craig is watching, I smile and wave to imaginary people on the dance floor who are neither waving nor smiling at me. It's important to feel popular when you are nervous.

Craig *was* watching me. As a matter of fact, he had spent the past half-hour mentally formulating a plan to convince me to come home with him. He predicted that it would take a while to get me to leave all of my friends, especially since we'd just met, but he was hopeful. We would dance, get to know each other, maybe go for a walk through D.C. and order some late night pizza. Then he'd ask if I wanted to see his new house.

He walked over to me, handed me a beer, and opened with:

Hey.

Oh, hey.

Having fun?

Yep, you?

Yeah. Getting tired, though. Thinking about heading home soon.

Kay. Let's go.

He had wasted a lot of time planning.

So we excitedly hailed a cab together, but when we arrived at his house, we discovered that neither of us had any money. So Craig asked the cabbie if he could leave me in the car for collateral while he went in and found some cash.

I remember thinking: Brilliant plan. He's hot *and* smart.

Unfortunately, when Craig got inside, all his buddies were still up partying, and he got a little distracted. Actually, somebody handed him a beer, and he promptly forgot all about me and the cabbie, which I couldn't really blame him for because after ten minutes of sitting in the cab, I couldn't remember what I was doing there either. In my drinking days, I was a lot like Dori from *Finding Nemo*: every moment was a brand-new adventure because I had no clue what preceded it. So I just figured that the cabbie was my new friend and he needed to talk. We chatted for about twenty minutes. Then somebody inside said to Craig, "Hey, who was that chick you were talking to at the last bar?"

Craig thought, *Hmmmm. Something about that question is ringing some sort of bell.* And then he REMEMBERED me in the cab! Isn't that romantic??? And he RAN out to get me. Then he gave the cabbie his money and rescued me, and it all felt very much like a fairy tale.

Happiness is low expectations paired with a short-term memory problem.

Craig apologized profusely for forgetting about me. I told him no worries, I understood completely. To make him feel better, I admitted that I had totally forgotten what I was doing in the cab in the first place. I also added that I may have forgotten his name a little bit. I later asked Craig if these admissions had felt like red flags in regard to my character. He said no, he just thought, *"This girl is cool. We have a lot in common."* The week before he had woken up early Sunday morning to find himself sprawled across the back seat of a cab at the National Zoo. He had a feeling I might be the kind of girl who understood problems like that. He was right. I was *just* that kind of girl.

So we smiled at each other and held hands and went into his house.

Out to Lunch

When we were newlyweds, I packed Craig's lunch for work each day. God knows I couldn't make dinner, so I thought lunch would be a nice consolation prize. Craig seemed to appreciate the gesture, and it made me feel wifely and loving and grown up.

One day Chase and I drove to Craig's office to meet his coworkers for lunch. Craig was waiting in the shiny lobby and proudly led us to the conference room, where clusters of pretty people in fancy suits waited to greet us. I was nervous because the room felt so different from the teachers' lounge at my school and because everyone was staring at us. But most of my anxiety came from my desperation to make Craig proud. Also, in situations like this, I always feel *very short*. Usually I start feeling taller and better when everyone sits down. But this time when everyone finally sat and started to eat, things got dramatically worse.

Most of Craig's coworkers carried their lunches in from restaurants. The women drank lattes or green teas and nibbled pastries from Starbucks and the men ate paninis or hoagies. The few who appeared to have brought their lunches from home carried their sushi rolls, chopsticks, and Evian in fancy patterned lunch packages that looked like mini-briefcases.

Craig, on the other hand, *their boss*, was beaming while using his brown paper sack that I had *decorated with rainbow hearts* as

73

a place mat on which he spread his four teeny triangles of peanut butter and jelly, string cheese, goldfish, fruit snacks, and *lemonade juice box*. I watched with horror as he fished out the index card on which I'd written, "To the best daddy in the world— We are so proud of you! Hugs and Kisses, Glennon and Chase." He read it, smiled, and slid the note into his pocket. I shuddered as I watched his huge fingers pry apart the string cheese's plastic wrapping and eat it in two bites, then rip off the teeny straw from the juice box, poke it into the little hole, and drink it all in one sip. He looked like a giant holding that juice box. Finally, to my utter dismay, he opened his *ocean animal fruit snacks* and tossed them into the air, one at a time, catching each one in his mouth.

I melted into my chair, willed my face to return to its original color, and tried to appear busy feeding Chase. Occasionally I glanced at Craig's face for signs of humiliation, but none was there. He just looked happy and, well, proud, actually. I was struck deaf and dumb. I gave up on making a good impression and just tried not to cry.

When Craig got home I greeted him with: *"Why didn't you tell me a year ago about grown-up lunches?* **Where does everyone learn these things?** *Did I miss some sort of class? What other basic life things do I not know? I want you to write them down for me, please. Right now."*

Craig looked surprised and then smiled and said, "I love your lunches."

I offered a halfhearted smile and then turned away to make our Easy Mac dinner.

That night I went into Craig's closet to put away his laundry and noticed a note taped to the inside of his door. It said, "To the best daddy in the world—we are so proud of you! Hugs and Kisses! Glennon and Chase."

Airing Our Dirty Laundry

Recently as I was walking up and down the grocery aisles, I noticed a distinct, mildewed, putrid odor in the air. I looked around for the responsible party, until I discovered that she was me. I stank.

When I got home, Craig came out of the house to help me with the groceries and I said, "Honey, smell me. I stink."

Craig sniffed my shirt and said without surprise, "Yes, you do."

And I said, "Well, what IS that? It's disgusting."

And Craig said the following: "It's mildew. All our clothes smell like that. We always stink."

I'll just give you a few seconds to digest that information. I know I needed a little time.

"What? Well why didn't you tell me, husband?"

"I was scared to tell you. You get sensitive about . . . house-keeping stuff."

"Oh. So allow me to clarify. You'd rather reek all day at work and allow Chase to be the *stinky kid in class* than risk me getting mad?"

"Yes. Yes, I would. Definitely."

I left the groceries on the counter and immediately drove back to the store to buy some fancy detergent, the kind that costs more than five dollars. I smelled them all until I found one that reminded me of flowers and every popular girl I'd ever met. Then I came back home and started washing each Old Navy T-shirt, Dora the Explorer panty, and pair of yoga pants in the house.

I learned two very important things that day, and I'd like to share them with you, just in case you are in the Laundry and Wife Remedial Classes, like I am.

#1. This is, apparently, how laundry works: say your laundry day is Wednesday. You cannot put the laundry in the washer on one Wednesday and then wait to put it in the dryer until the following Wednesday. **You must finish it all on the SAME Wednesday.** It's unfair but true. If you don't, your family will smell like dead mice.

#2. You must be sweeter to your husband so he is not afraid to tell you that your entire family reeks.

Housekeeping and marriage are complicated.

Initiation

Craig models part-time, and a few years ago, Circuit City hired him for a national campaign. It seemed like his face was all over the country for months. One weekend, we took Chase to the mall and popped into Circuit City to check out flat screens. Chase proceeded to lose his little mind. There were posters of Craig covering the walls and life-size Craig figures standing in every corner. Chase ran around pointing and hugging the figures and screaming, *"DADDY! DADDY!"* EVERYONE in the store, employees and shoppers, stopped and stared at Chase, Craig, and the posters, utterly confused. It was weird. Not particularly fun, even. Just weird.

We traveled to Ohio for New Year's Eve that year, like we do every year. Tisha's side of the family lives in Ohio, and my heart is there. Tisha has four sisters and two brothers. Collectively all these siblings made thirteen babies who became my first best friends. This loud, beautiful, closely knit, charmingly felonious crew was headed by Alice Flaherty and Bill Kishman, my grandma and grandpa. My grandpa was a gentle and wise surgeon who died twenty-five years ago. Alice is, quite literally, still kickin'. She is eighty-eight and remains the feistiest Irishwoman this side of Dublin. If you call her, she won't answer because she'll likely be in Vegas. Since she'll be busy shooting craps, you'll get her voice mail, which says, "I'm at the pub. Don't bother me. I'll call ya if I get back."

Over a half-century ago, she and my grandfather met at a bar near the hospital where he worked as a surgeon and she as a nurse. Alice was having a drink with her friends when Bill approached her shyly and said, "Excuse me, are you a nurse?" Alice looked at Bill, then down at her uniform and said, "No, Einstein. I'm a fireman." It was love at first fight. They shared a beautiful forty-year marriage based on the unspoken rule that Alice was allowed to continue to be, well, *Alice*. Along with the Flaherty passion and fury seems to come a lack of common sense. Basically the members of my family find sense to be too "common" for us. We are *above* sense, really.

One afternoon, Alice and my mother pulled into a parking garage and encountered a gate with a sign beside it that said, "Pull Up. Automatic Gate." Alice threw her hands in the air and said, *"Well, glory be to God. Why the hell would you have to PULL UP an automatic gate?"* She had the car in park and was outside trying to lift the gate herself before my mother understood what was happening.

Another time, Alice left for the mall—the mall that is five miles from her home, the mall that she'd been visiting regularly for forty years. A half an hour later, she pulled back into the driveway, and my uncle came out of the house to help her with her bags. She told him to *scram*, she'd come back because she'd gotten lost and she just needed to "start over." From her house.

That's just how it is. There's no need to argue or reason. Trying to reason with Alice proves nothing except that you've clearly not known her for long. It's best just to sit down and let her make you laugh. Don't try to fix a Flaherty. We do not think we're broken. We're thinking about more important things than how to navigate life gracefully. Alice and her descendants are soft places to land for folks who are wary of the self-help craze. My extended family is proof that there are plenty of folks who are just fine with the way they are, thank you very much. It's a little scary. But mostly refreshing.

When I was growing up, Ohio was heaven to me. Most of Tisha's sisters and brothers stayed in their home town to raise their families, and visiting them was the highlight of my childhood. The thirteen of us played all day in Grandma's pool. Exhausted at sunset, we'd dry off, eat pizza, and plan our sleepover. Our sleepovers never involved sleep. Caren and I were the oldest cousins. Caren was my hero. I thought she was the prettiest girl on the planet (she is). She and I would stay up until we saw the streetlights go out. Then, as the sun rose, we would sneak into the kitchen and pour thirteen bowls of Rice Krispies with mounds of sugar on top. I'm certain that my desire for a large family (and perhaps my sugar addiction) originated in my grandmother's kitchen, pouring Rice Krispies with Caren.

Caren's mom is my aunt Judy. Judy, like Alice, is what they call, *Something Else*. If Judy likes you, you've got it made. If she doesn't like you, you'd best be on your way. One more thing: if you're hungry, Judy's not your best bet. The Flaherty/Kishman gene that renders us useless at following directions obviously extends to recipes. No one in my family can cook. *No one,* and there are a lot of us.

One day, when Caren was a child, Judy decided to "make a cake." Before this day, Judy had never even decided to "make a sandwich." In fact, before this day, Judy had never even made *a purchase at the grocery store*. One might be tempted to assume that I am exaggerating. I am not. Grocery stores stress Judy out, and the women in our family try to make decisions that will keep us as calm as Irishly possible. But on this day, Judy was determined. Caren, who was ten years old, was to be her assistant. Poor Caren was terrified.

The cake Judy was determined to make was of the JELL-O No-Bake variety. So really, she was making, not baking, this cake. Judy poured the milk and the JELL-O powder into the crust and then picked up the box to read the next direction. She recited the following to Caren: "Step Three. Cover and tape the cake on the counter." Judy looked down at Caren's huge brown eyes, which were twitching in anticipation of impending calamity.

"Well, why are you just standing there? Go FIND SOME TAPE!"

Caren scurried away and ransacked the house. No tape.

Fearfully, she returned to Judy and said, "Mommy, I can't find any tape."

Judy said, "WELL. THEN. Go to Gramma's house and get some tape from her! HOW THE HELL IS ANYBODY SUPPOSED TO BAKE AROUND HERE WITH NO TAPE? GO!"

So Caren ran down the street, burst into my grandmother's house, and breathlessly demanded tape. My grandma asked her why she needed tape. Caren said, "We're trying to make a cake!" And my grandma said, "Oh. All right then, it's in the office." Because, you see, my grandmother has never made a cake in her life either and wouldn't have the slightest idea that tape is an unusual ingredient. So Caren grabbed the masking tape, ran all the way home, burst through the door, and yelled to her mom, "Mommy, I got the tape!" Judy called her over to the counter and told her to start taping. Judy and Caren used an entire roll of masking tape securing that cake to the counter.

When it was completely covered and secured beyond a shadow of a doubt, Judy picked up the box and read to Caren: "Step Four: Place cake in freezer."

Judy and Caren stared at the cake that they had just spent fifteen minutes taping to the counter.

Then Judy started using some very special language. Caren remembers that the tirade included loud requests for intersession from Jesus, Mary, and Joseph. At this point Caren picked up the cake directions with trembling hands, in hopes of finding a clue. After a moment and several silent prayers, Caren said in a teeny-weeny voice, "Mommy? Step three says cover and TAP the cake on the counter."

It's important to note these things because genetics are crucial. We cannot escape them. Which is what I told my friend Carrie when she found me trying to preheat her oven with a hair dryer. Preheat. *Heat before.* Totally logical, when you think about it. Actually, don't really think about it. Moving right along.

The point of all of this is that these are the people with whom we ring in every New Year. Each December, our entire extended family makes the pilgrimage to Uncle Keith and Aunt Stephanie's house in Ohio. Everyone comes. The thirteen of us have become thirty-four of us, including spouses and babies and fiancées and significant others. Our family New Year's Eve party is our touchstone—the one constant that we know, no matter what happens during the year, will be there waiting for us. There may be more of us or fewer of us, and our hearts might be fuller or emptier due to the year's happenings, but we will be there. Our family show will go on. Even the year that time stopped—the year Caren, Frankie, and Ali's daddy, Judy's husband, our Uncle Frank, died—we were there. We all cried as that reliable and relentless ball dropped, but we were there. What else is family if not a commitment to keep showing up?

Unfortunately, Craig and I couldn't make the New Year's trip in 2003 because I was nine months pregnant with Chase. So when we pulled up to Keith's house on December 31, 2004, it was the first time my little family was to meet my big family. I was busting with excitement. Craig was excited too, in a nervous sort of way. He'd heard the stories. Also, he was worried about what he'd eat. As we pulled up closer to Keith's house, we were startled by the strange, humongous statue spotlighted in the front yard. It was Craig—a ten-foot, three-dimensional tower made up of Craig's head. The tower was tied down with ropes and driven into the ground with wooden stakes and surrounded by five floodlights. Craig's face was as big and bright as the moon.

Craig shrank into his seat. I thought he might not get out. I told him the worst part was over; he just had to make it into the house and keep smiling. But I was wrong. So very wrong. When we walked into Keith's house, it became painfully obvious that Keith had *ransacked* his local Circuit City. Craig was *everywhere*. There were life-sized cutouts by the food table and blowups of his face above the sink. Craig's head peeked out from behind every toilet. There was *nowhere to go to get away from Craig's face*. There were more Craigs at the party than there were guests. It was absolutely phenomenal.

The best was yet to come. On New Year's Day, Keith woke Craig up at the crack of dawn and said that he needed help with an errand. Then he made Craig drive to the Cleveland Circuit City with him, walk into the store, *holding all the life-size cutouts of himself,* and return them. Keith had made a deal with the owner that he'd bring the Craig paraphernalia *and the Craig* back to return the signage. When they walked in the store, Uncle Keith tapped the poor teenage girl behind the counter, yanked Craig's hat off (which was pulled down close to his chin), and said, "HEY! DO YOU RECOGNIZE THIS GUY? DO YOU KNOW WHO THIS IS?"

The embarrassed girl's eyes widened and she said quietly that *Yes, she knew who he was.* She'd been staring at his face for months. Everyone was awkwarded into silence. Except for Keith. Keith was thrilled. Keith was beaming. Keith had been orchestrating this weird, thrilling moment for weeks, and here he stood, victorious.

These are the sorts of schemes and pranks that the men in my family *have* to execute or endure to counterbalance the Flaherty/ Kishman insanity. To distract themselves from the female drama, they create their own. And Craig endured. He even laughed. Now he's one of Keith's best accomplices. Today Craig would tell you that Uncle Keith is on his list of Top Ten Favorite People in the World.

That's the thing about becoming a family: you gotta melt. You have to keep melting into each other until you become something entirely new. The only constant family rule is that everyone has to keep showing up.

On Weaving and Repentance

Repentance is a fancy word used often in Christian circles. I don't use fancy religious words, because I don't think they explain themselves well. Also, fancy language tends to make *in* people feel more in and *out* people feel more out, and I don't think that's how words are best used. Words are best used to describe specific feelings, ideas, and hearts as clearly as possible—to make the speaker and the listener, or the writer and the reader, feel less alone and more hopeful.

I used to be annoyed and threatened by the word *repentance,* until I figured out what it really means to me. Repentance is the magical moment when a sliver of light finds its way into a place of darkness in my heart, and I'm able to see clearly how my jerkiness is keeping me from peace and joy in a specific area of my life.

Maya Angelou shined a light into the dark part of my heart where I keep my relationship with my mother-in-law. In her book, *Letter to My Daughter,* Angelou writes about a dinner party she attended during her first trip to Senegal at the home of a very rich and sophisticated friend. As Angelou explored the decadent home and observed the elegant guests, she noted that they were all carefully stepping around the beautiful, expensive rug in the middle of the floor to avoid dirtying it. She became appalled that her hostess would be so shallow as to value her things above her guests' comfort. Angelou decided to act; she stepped onto the rug and walked back and forth several times. The guests, who were "bunched up on the sidelines, smiled at her weakly." Angelou smiled back, proud that through her boldness they might also be "encouraged to admit that rugs were to be walked on."

She then joined the guests on the sidelines, her head held high. She had done what was right.

A few minutes later, the servants came out and quietly removed the rug from the floor, replacing it with an equally extravagant one. They then proceeded to carefully place the plates, glasses, wine, and bowls of rice and chicken on the new rug. Angelou's hostess clapped her hands and announced joyfully that they were serving Senegal's most beloved meal "for our Sister from America, Maya Angelou." She then asked all the guests to sit. Angelou's face burned.

She had dragged her dirty shoes all over her gracious hostess's tablecloth. Angelou concluded her story with this: "In an unfamiliar culture, it is wise to offer no innovations, no suggestions or lessons. The epitome of sophistication is utter simplicity."

When Craig and I were first married, I experienced his family as an unfamiliar culture. Communication was different, celebrations were different, mealtimes were different, and expressions of love were different. I found this to be unacceptable. To me, different meant wrong. I became offended and perpetually suspicious. In a million subtle and not-so-subtle ways, I tried to change my in-laws. I suggested new traditions. I offered advice. I found fault with their personalities and marriage and their relationships with their children and grandchildren. I dragged my dirty shoes all over my mother-in-law's tablecloth. The one she'd spent decades carefully weaving.

I imagine my refusal to accept my mother-in-law hurt her deeply, but she gave Craig and me time and space to work it out on our own. She bowed out. That must have been a hard decision, one I pray I never have to make with my own son. I pray that my future daughter-in-law will be wiser and kinder than I from the start. She probably won't be, though. She'll probably be just like me. She'll want to create her own weaving pattern, which might mean that she'll need to walk all over mine for a while.

As a young mother and wife, establishing a pattern that suited me was difficult. Learning to weave required all of my attention. I needed time and space to establish my own rhythm and style, and perhaps my rejection of the old patterns was necessary to the discovery of my own.

True repentance is messy, and it takes time, but that sliver of light is worth waiting for. And when it's real, it sticks. Thank you, Ms. Angelou, for leading me to repentance.

I'm not big on advice, mainly because most days I learn what an idiot I was yesterday. This is hopeful, because it means I'm moving in the right direction. But it also makes it risky to offer wisdom today. Even so, I feel safe suggesting this:

Mothers-in-law, enjoy watching your daughter-in-law learn to weave. When she makes a mistake, when she drops a stitch, allow her to notice it on her own. Tell her often how beautiful her pattern is. Be kinder than necessary. Bring her some tea. Be simple. Be sophisticated.

And *daughters-in-law,* notice the beauty of the rug that your mother-in-law spent a lifetime weaving. Remember that her pattern is mostly firmly established—no need to suggest improvements. Be kinder than necessary, being mindful that the piece of art it took her a lifetime to weave—*her masterpiece*—she gave to you, to keep you warm at night. One day you'll give your masterpiece away too. Be simple. Be sophisticated.

Sucker – On Vacuuming

A while ago, Craig came home with a new vacuum. An *unsolicited* new vacuum.

Like cooking, I consider vacuuming to be something that show-offy people do. And also people who are not quite as deep and sentimental as I am.

The floors in my home read like a history of our family. In that corner, you might find Cheerios from a special play-date last month, and under that rug you'll find glitter from last Thanksgiving's craft. It's lovely, really. Since I am incapable of ordering pictures or assembling family photo albums, Craig and I sit on the couch in the evenings, gazing from pile of floor crap to pile of floor crap, reminiscing. We find these moments to be quite special. But if you are the vacuuming type, I don't want you to feel guilty. I'm just suggesting that kids grow up fast, so you might want to consider setting aside some floor memories.

Several years ago, I started suspecting that my friends had different beliefs about vacuuming and memory keeping. It seemed they were opposed to using floors as scrapbooks, because their carpets always had those fancy *lines* in them. You know, those fresh, prideful, "I just vacuumed" lines? I began to feel a little uncomfortable about my unliney carpets. Now, one might predict that this discomfort would lead me to reevaluate my vacu-uming boycott, but one might predict wrong. I find my vacuum to be very heavy and ugly and not at all conducive to relaxing. There is nothing that leads me into a cursing tirade faster than trying to lug my vacuum up two flights of stairs. And Jesus said, *If your vacuum causes you to curse, gouge it out,* or something like that. So actually *becoming* a real-life vacuumer wasn't an option, since I love Jesus. If you *do* vacuum, I'm not trying to suggest that you *don't* love Jesus. I assume it's possible to do both. I'm just saying it's not *likely.* Not likely at all.

In any case, it was becoming clear that I needed to start think-ing creatively about this vacuuming issue.

One day I was watching Tish stroll her baby doll around the family room in a little pink baby stroller. My gaze fell to the floor behind her, and I noticed that the stroller wheels were making perfect lines across the carpet. *Perfect, fancy, "I just vacuumed" lines.* CA-CHING!

For the last three years, before company arrives, before Craig comes home from a trip, every time I feel like playing dutiful housewife, I call Tish and ask her if she'd like to take her baby for a walk. And Tish says, "A *reg-a-lar* walk or a *careful* walk, Mommy?" And I say, *"A careful walk, honey."* When she was two, I taught Tish that a *careful walk* is when you stroll your baby back and forth across the carpet in such a way that the stroller lines run perfectly parallel to each other . . . back and forth, back and forth, back and forth. And so for three wonderful years, Mommy sat on the couch and cheered for Tish while she and her baby doll "vacuumed."

Craig would come home and say, "Wow! You vacuumed!" with the same proud tone he uses when I cut a tomato all by myself. And I would smile and bat my eyelashes coyly but never answer directly because honesty is very important to me.

It was a miracle, really. Except that one night I saw Craig looking quizzically at the floor. I realized with terror that he was finally noticing the piles of floor crap surrounding my fancy lines. Not good.

I had anticipated that this might be the fly in the ointment, so I quickly mumbled something like "stupid vacuum's broken. But nice lines, huh? Look! *Shark Week* is on!" I have been mumbling variations of those sentences for three years now, with great success.

So when Craig walked in the house with this surprise vacuum, I was suspicious that he was suspicious. And so I watched his face *verrrry closely.* And right after he said, *"Look! This will make life so much easier! I hate for you go to all that trouble with that broken vacuum and never get the results you want,"* I noticed a faint smirk and an itty-bitty centimeter of an eyebrow-raise. It was almost imperceptible. But I saw it. My first thought was: *He **knows**. He knows about the stroller vacuuming. The jig is up.*

But I recovered quickly. And my second thought was: *Oh. The poor guy doesn't know who he's messing with here. He has grossly underestimated the depths to which I am prepared to sink to preserve my way of life. He just doesn't **know.***

The other day, after Craig left for work, I told Tish that I had a surprise for her. I announced that since she was such a *big girl* now, it had become time to pass down her itty-bitty baby stroller to Amma, because I had bought her a *brand-new, big girl stroller*. I explained that big girl strollers look very, very different from little girl strollers and even make big noises like cars! Because big girl strollers have *engines*.

Time for a *careful walk*, baby. Back and forth. Back and forth. *Your move, Hub-Dog.*

Easter

Craig and I never decided on "our song." Actually we might have, but since we were quite tipsy for a long while, we can't remember much. Plus, we had questionable judgment. So I'm quite sure that if we had a song during our courtship, it was likely one by Snoop Dogg or Britney Spears.

A few months ago, a friend sent me a link to a song and said that it reminded her of us.

I was so excited. Isn't it exciting to get a glimpse of who people think you are? Because, seriously, none of us really knows what we're like, do we?

I anxiously listened to the song. Well, really, I clicked on the link and couldn't get it to work and yelled and cried about how much I hate my computer until Craig ran downstairs to avoid property damage and gently moved the mouse and it worked immediately while I closely monitored his face for any traces of smugness. I hate this whole process, which repeats itself several hundred times a day.

Then we listened to the song. And I got chills. Craig and I replayed it maybe six times. We decided that John Prine must have been WATCHING THE TWO OF US when he wrote this song.

It's called "Spanish Pipedream," and it's about an unsuspecting guy who walks into a bar and meets a topless alcoholic dancer who has some strange ideas about life. And despite the fact that he should probably run, he marries her, because he thinks she might be on to something. Also, because, well, she's topless. Then they build a house in the country, kill their TV, and have a bunch of kids who eat peaches and find Jesus all by themselves.

Obviously, there are some important differences between us and the couple in the song. For example, we prefer pears to peaches. But the rest is dead-on.

Craig loved the song as much as I did, and he got teary and we decided that it was *our song*. We had a moment.

This is how I have been telling myself this story. But that night when we were getting in bed, Craig asked, "What are you writing about tomorrow?" and I responded, "Our song." Then he said, "What's our song?" I stopped what I was doing and looked at him very scary. He looked at me blank and terrified.

Then I started thinking back to what really happened that morning, and the replay looked very different. I remembered details like these: Actually, the whole time we were listening to the song, Craig was on his iPhone. And then I remembered his facial expression, which sort of suggested that he hated the song. And then I remembered how he kept saying, "awww," and "sure, honey," and "uh-huh" without looking up at all. Hmm. I wonder how many of my beautiful experiences are not really how I write them in my head? Whatever. I don't want to know. I try never to allow other people's lack of participation to get in the way of shared moments.

During the first nine years of my marriage, I rolled my eyes sweetly and laughed about this sort of communication break-down. *Boys will be boys,* you know. But lately I laugh about it less.

Craig and I have two recurring problems in our marriage. I feel sad when I don't get listened to, and Craig feels sad when he doesn't get made out with. I am starting to understand that these two problems are related. They're both about intimacy. Craig and I lack intimacy. When we talk, we seem to miss each other; it's like we're communicating on different planes. I'm high and low, and he's in the middle. We don't connect. And when we have sex, we don't really connect either.

Craig wants to be intimate physically, which feels odd and icky to me when I don't feel like we're being intimate anywhere else. If we are not connecting in the kitchen, in the family room, in the backyard, and at the dining room table, we're not really going to connect in the bedroom either. We're just going through the motions. But it seems to me like going through the motions is good enough for Craig. Like just getting the job done is sufficient. And that bothers me, a whole lot. I want *more* in *every* room of our house. And if I can't have real intimacy, then I don't want to fake it. *That* I can't tolerate.

To me intimacy is about communication. Through the written or spoken or physically expressed word, communicating is how we get into each other's hearts and minds.

An intimate friend is someone who notices when I'm saying something important and never forgets it. Each feeling, story, and secret is a gift. A good friend knows that, so she doesn't throw it away. She keeps my gifts in a special place and never loses them, so my energy and time feel well spent. In an intimate relationship, every conversation builds on the last, and what each has shared is what binds. Good friends become each other's keepers. I hold your story in my mind. I carry it for you. I'm a record of your life. I know what you will do next because I know what you've done in the past. We communicate paragraphs through a glance or a raised eyebrow. When our eyes connect and twinkle over a crowded table, I know telepathically that you are remembering the *very same thing at the very same moment*. In those moments, we are on the same page of each other's stories.

I have this telepathy with my intimate friends. This type of intimate friendship makes me feel safe and loved and known. It also makes me the lucky recipient of special gifts. Because when I talk to an intimate girlfriend, she not only listens and remembers the things I say; she stops and thinks and offers me something back. She tries to relate. She asks questions, because she really wants to understand. She gives feedback. At best, she offers her insight and, at the very least, humor and empathy. I have confidence in these friends, so I'm able to confide in them.

With Craig, it's different. Sometimes I tell him stories—stories that are really important to me—and he doesn't remember.

Craig probably doesn't know that when I was eight, I had two cats named Gummy and Blackie. When Gummy had kittens, she abandoned them in my bedroom closet, and I didn't find them until they were all dead but one. I called an all-night vet's office and they told me to feed the kitten with an eyedropper and buttermilk. I did just that, and I never left his side for days. I named him Miracle. Despite my hard work, he was a teeny bit brain damaged, so he'd attack everyone in our family but me. Which made me love him even more. He thought I was his mama. Three years later, Miracle got killed by a car right in front of my house.

Craig doesn't know the name of my family's old sailboat. He doesn't know who my best friend was in middle school or high school. He also doesn't know when my eating disorders started, and he couldn't tell you any of the details of my first AA meeting.

I've told him all these important things in the past. I've offered him these gifts before, but he loses them. It makes me feel like he's being careless, because these stories matter to me. They make up who I am. They make me different from anyone else Craig knows, and they make our relationship different from any other relationship he has. I have to ask: If you don't know my stories, if you don't know me, why do you love me? Me, personally. Not just your wife, but *me*?

Sometimes Craig really tries. He focuses and listens hard to what I'm saying. But even then, his replies seem canned to me. Flat. Like an answer from a Magic 8 ball. Whatever comes up, comes up. It seems like he's just trying to think of *what someone should say right now* instead of really reflecting and thinking and responding thoughtfully and honestly, like a girlfriend would.

The dangerous result of all the forgetting and canned responses is that I stopped sharing important things with Craig. I stopped offering him special gifts because the offerings felt like a waste of my time and breath. Like each day we were building sand castles that were washed away each night. So now we go through the motions, doing what a husband and wife are "supposed" to do. We talk for ten minutes daily; we make out a couple times a week. Check. Check. And I save my real stuff—my hard stories and worries and thoughts—for Sister, my parents, my girlfriends, and the blank page.

Is the Check, Check enough? Is wanting more too demanding? Am I asking my husband to communicate like a woman? Or is it sexist to suggest that a man can't get as deep and true as a woman can? And if it's not fair for me to expect Craig to be intimate with me mentally and emotionally, is it fair for him to expect physical intimacy from me? Because going through the motions in the bedroom, it's not working for me. It makes me feel used and resentful and angry.

And here's what happens:

I recoil from Craig's touch often. He hugs me, and I politely endure, looking over his shoulder at the unfinished dishes and the toys on the floor lying in wait to break my ankle. He stops me in the kitchen for a kiss, and I make sure, with broken eye contact and a friendly pat on the back, that this kiss, while not totally unappreciated, is a definitive dead end. I spend a lot of time making sure Craig knows that his affection is going nowhere. Affection feels like a means to an end to me, so I cut it short one way or another. Sometimes I start discussing my overwhelming exhaustion as soon as he walks in the door from work, setting the stage for rejection early, so there is no false hope.

On the nights when it's officially *been a while* and offering more excuses would signify that we really have a problem, he'll approach me, and I'll try to remain open. But then, very often, I start to feel angry.

Sometimes the anger is mild, like annoyance. I'm so tired after a long day with the kids, so used up, so saturated by need and touch already, *why must you be needy too?* Can't we just be grown-ups and do something practical? There's so much still to do: the laundry needs to be folded, the lunches packed, forms signed . . . miles to go before I sleep. Is there really time for something so *unproductive*? And really, we haven't talked, really *talked* for weeks. How does sex even *make sense*? How do you compartmentalize like that? Do you want *me*, or do you just want *sex*? That distinction makes all the difference. That distinction *is* intimacy.

But *intimately* is not how we learned to do it. Before marriage, with other people, we learned to do it irresponsibly, lightly, recreationally, indiscriminately, and desperately. Neither of us has unlearned that yet. For example, it is virtually impossible for us to make eye contact during sex. It feels way too real or too fake, I'm not sure which. Layered on top of these individual issues is the fact that since we don't yet have *emotional* intimacy, physical intimacy seems extra phony to me. Phony sex feels as deep as scratching somebody's itch.

So one Friday morning after Craig had forgotten a very important story I'd told him the night before, I woke up early and wrote everything you've just read. I sent it to him at work. It was time. The truth is important. My subject line said, "You might not want to read this on the fly."

Two hours later, I got this reply:

Dear Glennon,

That's the hardest thing I've ever had to read. So many emotions right now: confusion, depression, anger, not feeling worthy of our relationship or any relationship, not knowing what to do or where to start. When I read this I am trying to figure out what and why. What is the issue with me? Is it lack of long-term memory, short-term memory recall, concentration, distraction, stress, all of the above? And why? Why is this happening? Do I have issues with the fear of loss? Am I afraid you and the kids will leave so I don't let my guard down and get emotionally attached? Probably. In every relationship I've hit the "get out of Dodge" button when my significant other got close. Had thoughts about doing that before Chase was born too, but God had different plans, which I'm tremendously grateful for.

I've let you and us down, but I'm not going to give up. I love you too much for that. I will keep fighting until I get this right. I don't want to be the old Craig who runs when things get hard or when feelings get involved. I need to break the cycle, I need to face my fears, and work on not falling into the same patterns. I have read a few articles today about the statistics of children of adult divorced parents and it's troubling to say the least. I need help.

I am proposing a do-over. I want to sit down with you and re-hash out your life. I want to re-learn everything about you as if it's our first time together. I will take copious notes (don't laugh, I'm serious) to ensure I'm learning. I don't want to miss anything and I will study it as if preparing for a final exam. There's nothing more important to me in life than passing that final exam (which to me means a life-long intimately satisfied relationship with you). I can't go back in time to the things I missed in 2001 or even last week, but I want a do over. Can we start over?

Love, Craig

Yes, I said. *Yes, we can.*

> *And the day came when the risk to remain tight in a bud was more painful than the risk it took to blossom.*
> —*Anais Nin*

But things always get worse before they get better. Craig came home that night, and we couldn't even see each other for all the sadness and heaviness and anger and fear between us. We spent most of the evening avoiding eye contact and went to bed early. The next day was a family birthday. We would have a house full of guests celebrating with us. It was too late to cancel, although we both wanted to. Craig kept disappearing from the party, and when I finally found him hiding upstairs in the bathroom, I said, "Are you okay?"

He said, "No. I'm not okay. This is the worst day of my life. I feel so alone. You are all I have. But I want to be with someone who wants to be with me. And I'm afraid I'll never be who you want me to be. I'm afraid I should just let you go now. Because I feel like I'm trying out for a team I'm never going to make."

And he cried and cried. But I didn't cry, not at all. I didn't even feel tempted to cry, which scared me. I felt like I was watching Craig as a third party—a curious and sympathetic observer. Compassionate, but removed. That was the moment I realized that maybe some of our emotional intimacy issues were mine.

I picked up Craig's hand and said, "It'll be okay. We have to go, there are presents waiting to be opened." So Craig dried his eyes, and we went downstairs and cheered and clapped and sang and took lovely family pictures for Facebook.

The next day was Easter Sunday. We'd been too distracted to tell the kids the Easter story. No God this year. Just baskets filled with jelly beans and *hurry up let's get to church.*

Craig and I sat next to each at church the next morning and listened to our friend and pastor talk about Easter. She said that for Christians, Easter means that people can rise from the dead, and that relationships can, too. That even the bush that looks withered and brittle and lifeless can bloom, if given enough time, enough tending, enough love. A new season will come. There is always hope. What looks like the end might just be the beginning.

She said that Sunday might be right around the corner, but there is no fast forwarding through Friday and Saturday. The cross has to come before the resurrection. It's the way of the world. And unless you bear witness to the truth, unless you face it head on and choose to open your heart to the pain, you won't bear witness to the miracle either. If you run away from the crucifixion, you just might miss the resurrection.

But I'm learning that the pain, the struggle that comes before the resurrection, can be a long and excruciating process.

We started seeing a therapist, where, one day, not long ago, Craig delivered The News. The News that no spouse ever believes she'll hear, even though so many of us do. The News was that our lack of intimacy was due to the fact that there had been a major betrayal of our marital vows, long ago and repeatedly. The News confirmed what I had *felt* all along. It was verification that the distance between our bodies and hearts and minds was real from the beginning. The distance was created by a solid wall of lies built between us. I knew we didn't have the marriage we wanted and needed, but before The News, I didn't know why. I didn't know why we couldn't reach each other. The News opened my eyes wide, and hurt like hell.

I told Craig to move out of our home immediately and explained that I wouldn't speak to him until he went through an intensive treatment program. He went. He was awakened. He decided to fight for our family with his new self. His truthful, out in the light, whole self.

While he was gone, I decided to divorce him. Then I decided to forgive him. Then I decided to kill him. Then I decided to stop deciding things. I am learning to listen to the still, small voice telling me not to run—not today at least—and I am taking each day as it comes. One at a time. Carrying on.

I remember what our pastor said about Easter. That even the shriveled, lifeless bush can bloom. That Easter Sunday comes after Saturday; the Resurrection after the Crucifixion.

Craig and I are in the *Saturday* of our marriage right now. We've started the hard work of healing and waiting and grieving and raging and holding each other. When I want to turn away or run away, which is all the time, I remember what Adrianne told me the night I bought my new bicycle. *When you feel like you're falling,* she said, *steer into the fall. Lean into it instead of away, and you'll be all right.* My favorite thing about life is transformation, and I don't want to miss Craig's. As a Zen master once said to Geneen Roth, "Enlightenment is seeing one thing through all the way to the end."

I read somewhere that God sends us partners who are most likely to help us heal. This rings true to me. It's just that sometimes the healing is so hard that one or both partners can't take it, so somebody bails, or makes it impossible for the other partner to keep on loving. I understand this completely. Healing is so painful. Thankfully, when we turn away someone who would have helped us heal, God sends another. I don't think he punishes us. He gives us lots and lots of tries. God is Forever Tries. I think He sends our healing partners in all different forms, not just spouses. He sends sisters, girlfriends, strangers, authors, artists, teachers, therapists, musicians, and puppies until one or several partners stick. But if we want redemption, we have to let one stick, eventually. We have to sit through the pain long enough to rise again.

Last night Craig and I went out to dinner, just the two of us. We sat down and Craig pulled out a notebook and a pen. He said, "Okay, let's start from the beginning. I want to know everything. *Every little thing.* And I want you to know me. The real, honest me. We'll take it slow. . . . Where were your parents working before you were born? How did they meet again? I'm going to take notes and study them later. Don't make fun of me. I want us to know and remember everything about each other."

Happy Easter.

Unwind

There was a couple who'd been married for twelve years. The first two years were good, happy even, but then the kids came and work got hard and money got tight and the shine wore off each of them. She used to see strong and silent, but now she saw cold and distant. He used to see passionate and loving, but now he saw dramatic and meddling. They allowed themselves to become annoyed with each other, so they stopped being careful. They stopped *taking care of each other* because they decided they needed to look out for themselves.

The distance between them grew longer and deeper until it felt impossible to touch even when they were in the same room. One day she said to her girlfriend, *I just don't love him anymore,* and it felt terrifying and exciting to say. Then he said to his buddy, *I don't know if I ever loved her.* And their friends asked, *what about counseling?* But it all seemed tangled up too tight to try to unwind.

She got home from work one evening, fed the kids, and put them to bed. She was tired to the bone. He was late again. Late *again.* And even though he was late and the house was a mess, she knew that he would walk in the door, pour himself a glass of wine, and sit down at the kitchen table and relax. He'd sit and *relax.* She couldn't even remember what relaxing felt like. She was always either going like hell or sleeping. *Somebody* had to keep the family running.

She stared at his bottle of wine on the counter. Then her eyes wandered over to their wedding photo on the wall. *Clueless*, she thought. We were *clueless. But happy.* Look at us. We *were* happy. We were *hopeful.*

God, please help us, she said silently.

Then she walked over to the counter and poured his glass of wine for him. She put it next to his book on the kitchen table—the place he loved to sit and relax—and she went upstairs to sleep.

He tiptoed into the house fifteen minutes later. He knew he'd missed the kids' bedtime again, he knew she'd be angry again, and he prepared himself for her steely silence. He hung his coat and walked into the kitchen. He saw his glass of wine, and his book, and his chair pulled out for him. He stood and stared for a moment, trying to understand.

It felt as if she was speaking directly to him for the first time in a long, long while.

He sat down and drank his wine. But instead of reading, he thought about her. He thought about how hard she worked, how early she woke to get the kids to school and herself to the office. He felt grateful. He finished his wine and then walked over to the coffee maker. He filled it up and set the automatic timer. 5:30 a.m. It would be ready when she came downstairs. He placed her favorite mug on the counter. And then he walked upstairs and quietly slipped into bed next to her.

The next morning, she woke up and stumbled downstairs, exhausted, to the kitchen. She stopped when she heard the coffee maker brewing and stared at it for a few moments, trying to understand. It felt as if he was speaking directly to her for the first time in a very, very long while. She felt grateful.

That evening she allowed her arm to brush his as they prepared dinner together. And after the kids went to bed, she stayed up and they assumed their TV-viewing positions on the couch. He reached out for her hand. It was hard, but he did it. She felt her hand find his.

And things started to unwind. A little teeny bit.

Look. I know it's hard. It's all so damn hard and confusing and complicated and things get wound up so tight you can't even find the ends sometimes.

All I'm saying is that *somebody's* got to pour that first glass of wine.

Because love is not something for which to search or wait or hope or dream. It's simply something to *do*.

MULTIPLYING

Don't Carpe Diem

Every time I'm out with my kids, this seems to happen: An older woman stops us, puts her hand over her heart and says something like, "*Oh*— Enjoy every moment. This time goes by so fast." Everywhere I go, someone is telling me to *seize* the moment, *raise* my awareness, *be* happy, enjoy *every* **second**, etc., etc., etc.

I know that this advice comes from a good place and is offered with the very best of intentions. But I have finally allowed myself to admit that *it just doesn't work for me*. It *bugs* me. This CARPE DIEM message makes me paranoid and panicky. Especially during this phase of my life while I'm raising young kids. Being told, in a million different ways, to CARPE DIEM makes me worry that if I'm not in a constant state of profound gratitude and ecstasy, I'm doing something wrong.

I think parenting young children (and old ones too, I've heard) is a little like climbing Mount Everest. Brave, adventurous souls try it because they've heard there's magic in the climb. They try because they believe that finishing, or even attempting the climb, is an impressive accomplishment. They try because during the climb, if they allow themselves to pause and lift their eyes and minds from the pain and drudgery, the views are breathtaking. They try because even though it hurts and it's hard, there are moments that make it *worth the hard*. These moments are so intense and unique that many people who reach the top start planning, almost immediately, to climb again. Even though any climber will tell you that most of the climb is treacherous, exhausting, *killer*. That they *cried* most of the way up.

And so I think that if there were people stationed, say, every thirty feet along Mount Everest yelling to the climbers, *"ARE YOU ENJOYING YOURSELF!? IF NOT, YOU SHOULD BE! ONE DAY YOU'LL BE SORRY YOU DIDN'T! TRUST US!! IT'LL BE OVER TOO SOON!* **CARPE DIEM!**" those well-meaning, nostalgic cheerleaders might be physically thrown from the mountain.

Now I'm not suggesting that the sweet old ladies who tell me to ENJOY MYSELF be thrown from a mountain. They are wonderful ladies, clearly. But last week, a woman approached me in the Target line and said the following: *"Sugar, I hope you are enjoying this. I loved every single second of parenting my two girls. Every single moment. These days go by so fast."* At that particular point in time, Amma was wearing a bra she had swiped from the cart and sucking a lollipop she undoubtedly found on the ground. She also had three shoplifted clip-on neon feathers stuck in her hair. She looked *exactly* like a contestant from *Toddlers and Tiaras*. A losing contestant. I couldn't find Chase anywhere, and Tish was sucking the pen on the credit card machine WHILE the woman in front of me was trying to use it. And so I just looked at the woman, smiled, and said, *"Thank you. Yes. Me too. I am enjoying every single moment. Especially this one. Yes. Thank you."*

That's not exactly what I wanted to say, though.

When Dorothy Parker was asked if she loved writing, she replied, "No. But I love *having* written." What I wanted to say to this sweet woman was, "Are you *sure*? Are you sure you don't mean you love *having parented*?"

112

I love having written. And I love having parented. My favorite part of each day is when the kids are put to bed and Craig and I sink into the couch to watch some quality TV, like *Wife Swap,* and congratulate each other on a job well done. Or a job *done,* at least.

Every time I write something like this, readers suggest that I'm being negative. I have received this particular message four or five times: *G, if you can't handle the three you have, why do you want a fourth?* That one always stings, and I don't think it's quite fair. Parenting is hard. Just like lots of important jobs are hard. Why is it that the second a mother admits that it's hard, people feel the need to suggest that maybe she's not doing it right? Or that she *certainly* shouldn't add more to her load. Maybe the fact that it's so hard means she IS doing it right, in her own way, and she happens to be honest.

Craig is a software salesman. It's a hard job in this economy. He comes home each day and talks a little bit about how hard it is. But I don't ever feel the need to suggest that he's not doing it right, or that he's negative for noticing that it's hard, or that maybe he shouldn't even consider taking on more responsibility. And I doubt his colleagues come by his office to make sure he's ENJOYING HIMSELF. I'm pretty sure his boss doesn't peek in his office and say: *"This career stuff, it goes by so fast. ARE YOU ENJOYING EVERY MOMENT IN THERE, CRAIG???? THE FISCAL YEAR FLIES BY!! CARPE DIEM, CRAIG!"*

My point is this: I used to worry that *not only* was I failing to do a good enough job at parenting, but that I wasn't *enjoying* it enough. Double failure. I felt guilty because I *wasn't* in parental ecstasy every hour of every day and I *wasn't* MAKING THE MOST OF EVERY MOMENT like the mamas in the parenting magazines seemed to be doing. I felt guilty because honestly,

I was tired and cranky and ready for the day to be *over* quite often. And because I knew that one day, I'd wake up and the kids would be gone, and *I'd* be the old lady in the grocery store with my hand over my heart. Would I be able to say I enjoyed every moment? No.

But the fact remains that I *will* be that nostalgic lady. I just hope to be one with a clear memory. And here's what I hope to say to the younger mama gritting her teeth in line:

"It's helluva hard, isn't it? You're a good mom, I can tell. And I like your kids, especially that one peeing in the corner. She's my favorite. Carry on, warrior. Six hours 'til bedtime."

And hopefully, every once in a while, I'll add, *"Let me pick up that grocery bill for ya, sister. Go put those kids in the van and pull on up. I'll have them bring your groceries out."*

Clearly, **Carpe Diem** doesn't work for me. I can't even *carpe fifteen minutes in a row,* so a whole diem is out of the question.

Here's what does work for me:

There are two different types of time. Chronos time is what we live in. It's regular time. It's one minute at a time, staring down the clock until bedtime time. It's ten excruciating minutes in the Target line time, four screaming minutes in time-out time, two hours until Daddy gets home time. Chronos is the hard, slow-passing time we parents often live in.

Then there's Kairos time. Kairos is God's time. It's time outside of time. It's metaphysical time. Kairos is those magical moments in which time stands still. I have a few of those moments each day, and I cherish them.

Like when I actually stop what I'm doing and really *look* at Tish. I notice how perfectly smooth and brownish her skin is. I notice the curves of her teeny elf mouth and her almond brown eyes, and I breathe in her soft *Tishy* smell. In these moments, I see that her mouth is moving, but I can't hear her because all I can think is: *This is the first time I've really **seen** Tish all day, and my **God**—she is **so** beautiful.* Kairos.

Or when I'm stuck in Chronos time in the grocery line and I'm haggard and angry at the slow checkout clerk. But then I look at my cart and I'm transported out of Chronos. I notice the piles of healthy food I'll feed my children to grow their bodies and minds, and I remember that most of the world's mamas would kill for this opportunity. This chance to stand in a grocery line with enough money to pay. And I just stare at my cart. At the abundance. The bounty. Thank you, God. Kairos.

Or when I curl up in my cozy bed with my dog, Theo, asleep at my feet and Craig asleep by my side, and I listen to both of them breathing. And for a moment I think, *How did a girl like me get so lucky? To go to bed each night surrounded by this breath, this love, this peace, this warmth?* Kairos.

These Kairos moments leave as fast as they come, but I mark them. I say the word *Kairos* in my head each time I leave Chronos. And at the end of the day, I don't remember exactly what my Kairos moments were, but I remember I had them. That makes the pain of the daily parenting climb worth it.

If I had a couple Kairos moments, I call the day a success.

Carpe a couple of Kairoses a day.

Good enough for me.

A Little Advice

I don't believe in advice. Everybody has the answers right inside her, since we're all made up of the same amount of God. So when a friend says, *I need some advice*, I switch it to, *I need some love,* and I try to offer that. Offering love usually looks like being quiet, listening hard, and letting my friend talk until she discovers that she already has the answers. Since I don't offer advice, Craig and I find it funny that people ask me for it every single day. Craig once asked what I make of that, and I told him that I think friends ask me for advice because they know I won't offer any. People need a safe place and some time to discover what they already know. So I just try to hold space and time for folks.

Recently, a dear friend called during a very hard day. She had made a parenting mistake. A parenting mistake is doing something opposed to what you believe is best for your children. I have a friend who is very health conscious and would call four frozen pizzas a horrible mistake, while I just call it dinner. Parenting mistakes are different for each mama. So when a friend tells me she made a mistake, I don't measure it against my beliefs and say: *OH PUH-LEASE. **THAT'S NOT A MISTAKE. I'LL TELL YOU WHAT A MISTAKE IS, MISSY.*** Competing about who's the worst is as much of a drag as competing about who's the best.

In this particular case, my friend had become tired and hopeless and spanked her child. She considered this a mistake because she doesn't believe in spanking. Please, baby Jesus, let us not debate the spanking issue. It's a mistake for some and not for others. This particular friend, who is as precious as water in a desert, was devastated. She asked me for advice. I immediately switched that to a request for love.

I told her what I do when I make a big or little parenting mistake, which is several hundred times a day. I try to remember two things:

#1. Who I am
#2. My most important parenting job

First, I remember that I am a human being, and human beings make mistakes. Almost constantly. We fall short of what we aim for, always. We get impatient. We get angry. We get selfish. We get extremely sick and tired of playing pet store. That's okay. It's just the way it is. We're human. Can't fight it. Elephants gotta be elephants and people gotta be people.

Then I remember what my most important parenting job is, and that is to teach my children how to deal with being human. Because most likely, that's where they're headed. No matter what I do, they're headed toward being messed-up humans faster than three brakeless railroad cars.

There is really only one way to deal gracefully with being human, and that is this:

Forgive yourself.

It's not a once-and-for-all thing, self-forgiveness. It's more like a constant attitude. It's just being *hopeful*. It's refusing to hold your breath. It's loving yourself enough to offer yourself a million more tries. It's what we want our kids to do every day for their whole lives, right? We want them to embrace being human instead of fighting against it. We want them to offer themselves grace. Forgiveness and grace are like oxygen: we can't offer it to others unless we put our masks on first. We have to put our grace masks on and breathe in deep. We have to show them how it's done. We need to love ourselves if we want our kids to love themselves. We don't necessarily have to love them more; we have to love *ourselves* more. We have to be gentle with ourselves. We have to forgive ourselves and then . . . oh my goodness . . . find ourselves sort of awesome, actually, *considering the freaking circumstances*.

A parenting magazine recently asked me to write an advice column for them. *About what?* I asked. *About raising happier kids,* they answered. *Jeeeeez,* I said. *I don't know. I think the kids are all right. I'd rather help make mamas happier.*

It's a good point, they said.

I just want us to remember that when we became parents, we didn't change species. We're still humans. I mean, we're bad-ass humans, for sure, but humans nonetheless. We make mistakes, all day, and that's good. We want our children to see that. We want them to learn how to handle mistakes because that's an important thing to learn. We expect to make mistakes, we say we're sorry, we forgive ourselves, we shrug and smile, and we try again.

Repeat.

Repeat.

Repeat.

Parenthood and God are Forever Tries.

Brave Is a Decision

Dear Chase,

Tomorrow is a big day. Your first day of third grade— *wow*.

When I was in third grade, there was a little boy in my class named Adam. Adam looked a little different, he wore funny clothes, and sometimes he even smelled strange. Adam didn't smile. He hung his head low, and he never looked at anyone at all. Adam never did his homework. I don't think his parents reminded him like yours do. The other kids teased Adam often. Whenever they did, his head hung lower and lower and lower. I never teased him, but I never told the other kids to stop either.

I never talked to Adam, not once. I never invited him to sit next to me at lunch, or to play with me at recess. Instead, he sat and played by himself. He must have been very lonely.

I still think about Adam. I wonder if Adam remembers me. Probably not. I bet if I'd asked him to play, just *once,* he'd still remember me.

I think that God puts people in our lives as gifts to us. The children in your class this year, they are some of God's gifts to you. So please treat each one like a gift from God. Every single one.

Baby, if you see a child being left out, or hurt, or teased, part of your heart will hurt a little. Your daddy and I want you to trust that heartache. Your whole life, we want you to notice and trust your heartache. That heartache is called *compassion,* and it is God's signal to you to *do something.* It is God saying, ***Chase! Wake up! One of my babies is hurting! Do something to help!*** Whenever you feel compassion, be thrilled! It means God is speaking to you, and that is magic. It means he trusts you and needs you.

Sometimes the magic of compassion will make you step into the middle of a bad situation right away.

Compassion might lead you to tell a teaser to *stop it* and then ask the teased kid to play. You might invite a left-out kid to sit next to you at lunch. You might choose a kid for your team first who usually gets chosen last. These things will be hard to do, but you can do hard things.

Sometimes you will feel compassion, but you won't step in right away. That's okay too. You might choose instead to tell your teacher and then to tell us. We are on your team—we are on your whole class's team. Asking for help for someone who is hurting is *not* tattling; it is *doing the right thing.* If someone in your class needs help, please tell me, baby. We will make a plan to help together.

When God speaks to you by making your heart hurt for another, by giving you compassion, just do *something.* Please do not ignore God whispering to you. I so wish I had not ignored God when he spoke to me about Adam. I remember him trying, I remember feeling compassion, but I chose fear over compassion. I wish I hadn't. Adam could have used a friend, and I could have too.

Chase, we do not care if you are the smartest or fastest or coolest or funniest. There will be lots of contests at school, and we don't care if you win a single one of them. We don't care if you get straight As. We don't care if the girls think you're cute or whether you're picked first or last for kickball at recess. We don't care if you are your teacher's favorite or not. We don't care if you have the best clothes or most trading cards or coolest gadgets. We just don't care.

We don't send you to school to become the best at anything at all. We already love you as much as we possibly could. You do not have to earn our love or pride and you can't lose it. That's done.

We send you to school to practice being brave and kind.

Kind people are brave people. *Brave* is not something you should wait to feel. Brave is a decision. It is a decision that compassion is more important than fear, than fitting in, than following the crowd. Trust me, baby, it is. *It is more important.*

Don't try to be the best this year, honey. Just be grateful and kind and brave. That's all you ever need to be.

Take care of those classmates of yours, and your teacher too. You *Belong to Each Other*. You are one lucky boy with all of these new gifts to unwrap this year.

I love you so much that my heart might explode. Enjoy and cherish your gifts. And thank you for being my favorite gift of all time.

Love, Mama

Whatever, Honestly

I take the kids to the gym regularly. My Lyme disease doesn't permit me to work out anymore, but I would never allow that minor detail to keep me from free child care. So I drop off the kids in the nursery and I sit in the sauna and read. It's exactly like hot yoga, without the parts of hot yoga that I resent, like the *moving* part and the *not allowed to read during* part. When I come out, I am smarter. And warmer. And more peaceful. So now instead of meeting on the exercise bikes and sitting still and talking, Adrianne and I meet in the sauna and sit still and talk. And when we leave, we are so sweaty that *we* even believe we've worked out.

Recently, following a particularly dramatic mommy meltdown, I bought some new workout clothes for my sauna exercise regimen.

Let me explain.

Once a week I have a breakdown during which I wail to Craig that for various reasons that I am too overwhelmed and despondent and incoherent to discuss in detail, my life is completely unmanageable. We call it a Mommy Meltdown in our home. My friend Erin calls it a *Caretaker Fatigue Attack*. Either way, mine include lots of tears and dramatic phrases thrown around, my favorite of which is: *I JUST CAN'T **TAKE IT ANYMORE***. Craig once made the mistake of asking me what specifically the

IT is that I am unable to **TAKE**, and let us just say that he will not make that mistake again.

Often, as I start to cool off from a meltdown, I decide that the only thing that will improve my life is to leave the house *alone*— immediately—and buy lots of crap. I do not know why this is my solution, but when I arrive at whatever crap store to which my van drives, there are always many other maniacal-looking women also wandering the aisles aimlessly. So I must not be the only one who considers crap-buying a viable solution to: *I JUST CAN'T TAKE IT ANYMORE!!!*

On my last crap-buying trip, I purchased some new workout (sauna) clothes. One piece was a yoga top with massive pads in the bra. *Pads in the bra.* The irony of practicing yoga in order to connect with the universe and one's inner self and find acceptance and self-love *in a padded bra* is not lost on me. As a matter of fact, it is *so me.* I bought two. I wore one of my new booby tops to the gym.

After doing my time in the sauna, I wasn't ready to leave yet, so I went out to walk on the treadmill. I smiled at the lady next to me and noticed that she was staring at me. I assumed that she was impressed by my huge boobs. I smiled humbly. The lady locked eyes with me and said, "Excuse me, your tag is still on."

Please understand that to me, this is like someone saying, "Excuse me, do you have the time?" No biggie. I **always** leave my tags on. Taking them off is just one of those things with which I can't be bothered. And since *I JUST CAN'T **TAKE IT ANY-MORE*** quite often, I have a lot of tags.

I thanked the nice woman and continued walking. I didn't look for the tag, didn't even pretend to. *I got 99 problems, lady, and a tag ain't one.*

A half-hour later I was back in the locker room preparing to shower. Yes, I shower at the gym too. I refuse to retrieve my children until we have reached the full two-hour nursery maximum. If I arrive three minutes early, I wait outside the door and stare into space for three minutes.

So I walked past the locker room mirror and did a double-take. Here's the tag. Here's the tag I was wearing, just like this, for my entire two hours at the *very crowded* gym.

And there you have it.

One, Two, Three

When the doctor places your firstborn in your arms, you hold your breath. You bring him home understanding that the Universe has made a mistake, that someone more qualified and motherly will show up to retrieve him soon. To pass the terrifying time, you play house. You hold him with trembling, clutching, sweaty hands. You still do. Your love for him is colored by fear because you are afraid he will die any minute. You do not trust that he can navigate his world. You eye his doctors, his playmates, his teachers, even his grandparents with great suspicion. Will they be gentle enough with him? He is so *sensitive*.

What you really mean is: *I am so sensitive. I'm like Lazarus, fresh from the tomb, eyes burning from the sun's brightness. I can't handle the ferocity and fragility of this new love. Please be careful with us.*

You're sure if you just hold his hand tight enough, read the right books, choose the healthiest foods, enroll him in the best schools, just hold your breath forever, he'll be *okay*. You're not sure what *okay* is anymore. Maybe okay means you'll succeed at keeping him and the world apart forever. Maybe okay just means that you'll both survive this love, this love so intense it threatens to consume you like a fire.

Holding your second child, you start to breathe again. You are elated and concerned. Your firstborn is replaced. You can't look at or listen to both of your babies at the same time. So you look *at* your baby while talking *about* your firstborn. You say, *hold on, honey,* all day. Your guilt is relentless. How will you convince them that they are each the center of your universe? This new angel seems like a stranger at first, and then your firstborn does. Suddenly he is some sort of giant. You wonder when he'll start pulling his weight already. You are worried you'll never find your balance. What is the right division of time, love, attention, fear, and worry? For the first time, you become concerned with how the juggling act you're attempting to perform appears to the world. *Am I doing it right? Am I saying the right things? Am I buying the right diaper bag, house, car, invitations? Are they wearing the right clothes? Am I? Do I appear to be enjoying motherhood enough???*

But then again, you have your moments, don't you? When they smile at each other, when he retrieves her toy, touches her hair, tickles her feet. When you hear two giggles coming from the family room for the first time. When you and your partner look at the two of them on the floor and exchange a glance that means, *Look at what we did. We're doing it. We're making a family.*

Then the third arrives. And as you hold her for the first time, you notice that your hands are steady and you're breathing easy. The all-consuming fire is gone. Love is just . . . love. You don't feel threatened anymore by her or the world. Because all of a sudden you see in her teeny little face that she *is* the world. And you understand that you're not her protector anyway; she has One of Those. You're just her teacher. You're just borrowing her for a little while. You decide not to spend so much of your precious time begging God to shield her from the world. Seems silly, all of a sudden. Because she, God, the world, they are all mixed up together inside that new skin.

Then, as you count her tiny fingers with yours, you check your heart and find no guilt there. Because you understand that you are about to present your older children with the greatest gift of their lives. Who else but a sibling travels with you from the start of life's path to the bitter end? And you know, now, that if your first and second born spend the next few months relearning that They're Not the Center of the Universe, well, good then. It's an important thing to know, and it's a lesson best learned early. So there's another gift to them, courtesy of you, and this littlest one.

You understand that things will get tougher when she comes home. You will sweat and curse more at the grocery store. You will have less money to buy her the right things. You will look far less graceful at playdates. But you will care less. Because you have listened to and spoken to enough honest parents to understand that we're all in this together. And that there is no prize for *most composed*. So you've decided to stop making parenthood harder by pretending it's not hard.

You look down at her, your third, and you think, *what's so different about you?* But before you finish asking the question, you know the answer. And your heart says to hers: *Oh. You're not different from the other two. I am. I'm learning how to love without so much fear. How to relax a bit, in this brutiful world. How to let go and trust. You are helping me breathe easier, you three. One at a time, and together.*

Amma, you came to me and you said. *It's okay, Mama. We're all going to be okay.*

I didn't know that before you told me, baby girl. I really didn't know.

Rejoicing

I get very anxious about Chase being away at school for eight hours each day. I would be more anxious if he were *home* eight hours a day, but still. That's the thing about parenting: anxious if you do, anxious if you don't. Every time I see that boy walk home from school I feel like Geppeto. Oh my *God,* I think. *Look at him! He moves. He walks! He's ALIVE!* Chase is a miracle I want to protect.

When I was in elementary school, all of these little things happened to me that made me embarrassed, or confused, or sad. Like when I had to stand against the huge cafeteria wall with my nose pressed against the big purple painted grapes, or when all the girls teased me at my lunch table because my hair was greasy. *You could start a car with all that grease,* they said. Or when the boys never chased me at recess. Or when a classmate brought a *Playboy* to school. Or when my friend Jennifer called me a *gay wad.* What's a gay wad? But these things didn't seem big enough to talk about, and I didn't want my parents to know that all wasn't perfect, so I kept sad and confusing things secret. And keeping secrets became second nature to me, which didn't work out so well for a couple of decades.

So when it comes to how my kids are doing at school, I don't worry about academics. I worry about social things. I worry about their time at lunch, at recess, and on the bus. Mostly children learn

133

to read and add and sit still *eventually*. But not everybody learns that he and others deserve to be treated with respect. Not everybody learns that he is OKAY and loved and precious and that it's all right to feel hurt and all right to hurt others, as long as he apologizes and tries to fix what he broke. Not everybody learns that different is beautiful. And not everybody learns to stand up for himself and others, even when it's scary. Eight is young to navigate a big social sea all by oneself. Thirty-six feels too young sometimes.

So last week, I snuggled in bed with Chase and told him all about the embarrassing, sad, scary little things that happened to me in elementary school. I told him that I never gave Bubba and Tisha a chance to help me, because I kept my worries in my heart. And by keeping my worries secret, they became problems. I told him that this was a shame, because the beautiful thing about being a kid is that you don't have any problems. You might have worries, but if you share those worries with your parents, they don't have to become problems. I told him that his daddy and I are his team. That his worries are really *our* worries, and that the most important thing in the world to us is his heart.

I explained to Chase that every night, he and I were going to lie in bed together and try to remember any sadness or worries that he had during the day. I told him that we were going to talk about them and then ask God to help us with them. Then he'd be able to relax and sleep soundly, knowing that God and Mommy and Daddy were *on* it.

I've learned a lot about my little boy while we've cuddled and remembered his worries.

For example, Chase thought that the first few weeks of school were a "tryout," and if he wasn't perfect, he could get cut. I was tempted to let him keep believing that one.

And the reason he always wants his dad to take him to baseball practice is that I embarrass him by cheering for everybody whether he hits the ball or not. *You're not supposed to cheer and yell "THAT'S OKAY" when people drop the ball, Mom. It's NOT GOOD to drop the ball. I don't know if you really understand baseball, Mom.*

Also, there's an older girl on the bus who's a bit of a bully, and Chase is scared of her. I told him that on Monday, his job was to find out what color her eyes were. That's all. *Just find out what color her eyes are, Chase.* Chase came home yesterday and said, *"MOM! Her eyes are BLUE! But listen, while I was looking at her eyes to find out what color they are for you, she quit her mean face and looked away! And she didn't look at me mean the rest of the bus ride! And then on the way home, she didn't look at me at all! She just passed right by!"*

Yep. Always look them in the eye, buddy. Mean can't handle the truth.

I think this worry talk is a ritual worth keeping. Because if we empty our hearts every night, they won't get too heavy or cluttered. Our hearts will stay light and open with lots of room for good new things to come.

A Mountain I'm Willing
to Die On

Along with every other concerned parent, I watch America's responses to bullying-related suicides closely. People always seem quite shocked by the cruelty that's happening in America's schools. I'm baffled by their shock, and I'm concerned about what's *not* being addressed in their proposed solutions.

The acceptable response seems to be that we should better educate students and teachers about what bullying is and how to react to it appropriately. This plan is positive, certainly. But on its own, it seems a little like bailing frantically without first looking for the hole in the boat.

Each time these stories are reported, the sound bite is: "kids can be so cruel." This is something we tend to say: *kids these days, they can be so cruel.* But I think this is just a phrase we toss around to excuse ourselves from facing the truth. I don't think kids are any crueler than adults. I just think kids are less adept at disguising their cruelty.

I heard a radio report that students who are most likely to be bullied are gay kids, overweight kids, and Muslim kids.

Hmmmmm.

I bet that at this point in American history, gay adults, overweight adults, and Muslim adults feel the most bullied as well.

Children are not cruel. Children are mirrors. They want to be "grownup," so they act how grown-ups act when we think they're not looking. They do not act how we *tell them to act at school assemblies*. They act how we *really* act. They believe what we believe. They say what we say. And we have taught them that gay people are not okay. That overweight people are not okay. That Muslim people are not okay. That they are not equal. That they are to be feared. And people hurt the things they fear. We know that. What they are doing in the schools, what we are doing in the media—it's all the same. The only difference is that children bully in the hallways and the cafeterias while we bully from behind pulpits and legislative benches and sitcom one-liners.

People are sensitive. People are heartbreakingly sensitive. If enough people tell someone over and over that he is not okay, he will believe it. And one way or another, he will die.

So how is any of this surprising? It's quite predictable, actually. It's trickle-down cruelty.

I don't know much. But I know that each time I see something heartbreaking on the news, each time I encounter a problem *outside,* the answer to the problem is *inside.* The problem is *always* me and the solution is *always* me. If I want my world to be less vicious, then I must become more gentle. If I want my children to embrace other children for who they are, to treat other children with the dignity and respect every child of God deserves, then I had better treat other adults the same way. And I better make sure that my children know beyond a shadow of a doubt that in God's and their father's and my eyes, they are okay. They are loved as they are. Without a single *unless.* Because the kids who bully are those who are afraid that a secret part of themselves is not okay. To that end, I wrote this letter to my son:

Dear Chase,

Whoever you are, whoever you become, you are loved. You are a miracle. You are our dream come true.

Chase, here is what would happen in our home if one day you were to tell your father and me that you are gay.

Our eyes would open wide.

Then we would grab you and hold you tighter than you would be able to bear. And while we were holding you, we would say a silent prayer that as little time as possible passed between the moment you knew you were gay and the moment you told us. And we would love you and ask you one million questions, and then we would love you some more and finally, I would rush out to buy some rainbow T-shirts, honey, because you know Mama likes to have an appropriate outfit for every occasion.

And I don't mean, Chase, that we would be *tolerant* of you and your sexuality. If our goal is to be *tolerant* of people who are different than we are, Chase, then we really are aiming quite low. Traffic jams are to be tolerated. People are to be celebrated. Every person is Divine. And so there would be celebrating. Celebrating that you had stepped closer to matching your outsides with your insides—to being who you are. And there would be a teeny part of my heart that would leap at the realization that I would forever be the most important woman in your life. Then we would tell everyone. We would not concern ourselves too much with their reactions. There will always be party poopers, baby.

Honey, we've worried that since we are Christians, and since we love the Bible so much, there might come a day when you feel unclear about our feelings about this, since there are parts in the Bible that appear to discuss homosexuality as a sin. Let us be clear about how we feel, because we have spent years of research and prayer and discussion deciding.

Chase, we don't believe that homosexuality is a sin. The Bible was inspired by God, but it was written, translated, and interpreted by imperfect people just like us. This means that the passing of this sacred scripture from generation to generation and from culture to culture has been a bit like the "telephone game" you play at school. After thousands of years, it's impossible to judge the original spirit of some scripture. We believe that when in doubt, mercy triumphs judgment. So your parents are Christians who study and pray and then carefully choose what we follow in the Bible, based on whether or not it matches our understanding of Jesus's overall message. Certainly we make mistakes. Everyone does. But it's our duty to try. We must each work out our own faith with fear and trembling. It's the most important thing we'll ever do. Even so, some folks will tell you that our approach to Christianity is scandalous and blasphemous. But honey, the only thing that's scandalous about this approach is admitting it out loud. The truth is that every Christian is a Christian who chooses what he follows in the Bible.

Recently there was some talk in my Bible study about homosexuality being sinful. I quoted Mother Teresa and said, "When we judge people we have no time to love them." I was immediately reprimanded for my blasphemy by a woman who reminded me of 1 Corinthians 6:9–10. But I was confused because this woman was speaking. In church. And she was also wearing a necklace. And I could see her hair, baby. She had *no head covering*. All of which are sooooo totally against the New Testament Bible Rules. And so I assumed that she had decided not to follow the parts of the Bible that limited *her* particular freedoms, but to hold fast to the parts that limit the freedoms of others. I didn't point this out at the time, because she wasn't a bad person. People are doing the best they can, mostly. It's best not to embarrass anyone.

Much of the Bible is confusing, but the most important parts aren't. Sometimes I wonder if folks keep *arguing* about the confusing parts so they don't have to get started *doing* the simple parts. So a long time ago, your father and I decided that if a certain scripture turns our judgment outward instead of inward, if it requires us to worry about changing others instead of ourselves, if it doesn't help us become better lovers of God and life and others, if it distracts us from what we are supposed to be doing down here—finding God in everyone, feeding hungry people, comforting the sick and the sad, giving whatever we have to give, and laying down our lives for our friends—then we assume we don't understand it yet, and we get back to what we do understand. Chase, what we do understand is that we are reborn. And here is what I believe it means to be reborn:

The first time you're born, you identify the people in the room as your family. The second time you're born, you identify the whole world as your family. Christianity is not about joining a particular club; it's about waking up to the fact that we are all in the same club. Every last one of us. So avoid discussions about who's in and who's out at all costs. *Everybody's in, baby*. That's what makes it beautiful. And hard. If working out your faith is not beautiful and hard, find a new one to work out. And if spiritual teachers are encouraging you to fear anyone, watch them closely, honey. Raise your eyebrow and then your hand. Because the phrase repeated most often in that Bible they quote is *Do Not Be Afraid*. So when they tell you that gay people are a threat to marriage, honey, *think hard*.

I can only speak from my personal experience, but I've been married for ten years and *barely any gay people* have tried to break up my marriage. I say *barely any* because that Nate Berkus is a little shady. I am defenseless against his cuteness and eye for accessories. He is always convincing me to buy beautiful trinkets with our grocery money, and this drives your sweet father a bit nuts. So you might want to keep your eye on Berkus. But with the exception of him, I'm fairly certain that the only threats to your father's and my marriage are our pride, insecurity, anger, and wanderlust. *Do not be afraid* of people who seem different from you, baby. Different always turns out to be an illusion. Look hard.

Chase, God gave you the Bible, and he also gave you your heart and your mind, and I believe he'd like you to use all three. It's a good system of checks and balances he designed. Prioritizing can still be hard, though. Jesus predicted that. So he gave us this story: A man approached Jesus and said that he was very confused by all of God's laws and directions and asked Jesus to break it down for him. He asked, "What are the most important laws?" And Jesus said, "Love God with all your heart, mind and soul, and love others as yourself." He added that every other scripture hangs on this one. So use that ultimate command as a lens to examine all other scripture. And make damn sure that you are offering others the same rights and respect that you expect for yourself. If you do that, you can't go wrong.

Chase, you are okay. You are a child of God. As is everyone else. There is nothing that you have done or will do that will make God love you any more or any less. Nothing that you already are or will become is a surprise to God. Tomorrow has already been approved.

And so, baby, your father and I have only one expectation of you. And that is that you celebrate others the way we celebrate you. That you remember, every day, *every minute*, that there is no one on God's Green Earth who deserves more or less respect than you do, My Love.

"He has shown you what is good. And what does the Lord require of you? To act justly and to love mercy and to walk humbly with your God."—Mica 6:8

Love, Mama

PS. We thought we should mention, honey, that if you're straight, that's okay too. I mean, it'd be a little anticlimactic now, honestly. But your father and I will deal.

PPS. As Daddy read this, I watched his gorgeous face intensify. He teared up a little. Then he slammed the letter down on the kitchen table and said emphatically and without a touch of irony, "DAMN **STRAIGHT.**" Which, when you think about it, is really the funniest thing Daddy could have said.

On Fish and Heaven

O ur family's first brush with death occurred when Chase's fish, Jacob, died. We had several beta fish over the years, and we'd replace each of the deceased without a single tear from the kids. But Jacob was special. He swam around in Chase's room for two years and survived a million sticky fingers and more than a few missed meals. Jacob kept an eye on things for us. We thought him very wise and responsible. I once admitted to the kids that I loved Daddy more than Jacob, and they were so hysterically horrified that I was forced to recant and promise that I did, in fact, love Daddy and Jacob exactly the same. Jacob was one of us.

We decided to tell the kids about Jacob's death right away so that there were no accidental surprises. All three children were playing together in the family room, so Craig and I sat down near them and I said, "We have some very sad news, guys." Their bodies froze and their little heads swiveled toward me. I said solemnly and quietly, "Jacob died this morning." I had resolved not to try to soften the blow by explaining it away prettily.

Tish immediately started to sob. I picked her up off the floor and she buried her face into my hair and curled into a teeny ball of self-preservation, like a roly-poly. Chase quickly covered his mouth with his hand, but not before I noticed the hint of a grin that curled his lips. This nervous grin is his first line of defense. He asked if he could see Jacob. I moved Tish to Craig's lap while Amma, looking concerned, waddled over to Tish and patted her curls lovingly, then whacked her hard on the forehead and grinned. Tish's whimper turned into a wail. Craig and I shot each other good luck glances, and I followed Chase up the stairs to view the body.

Chase walked into his room and marched like a soldier directly to the tank. When he saw Jacob's lifeless body, he noticed that his friend's vibrant red color had faded to gray. He asked why, but he didn't wait for an answer. He just covered his eyes with his little second-grade hands so that finally the tears could come. They streamed down his cheeks as his shoulders fell and shook, and he crumbled into me.

I wanted so badly to tell Chase that it was *okay*, that we would replace Jacob with a new fish, a bigger fish, a whole *school of fish,* but I didn't. This was his first experience with death, and I wouldn't suggest to him that death can be cheated through replacement. I wouldn't teach him that pain should be avoided, dodged, or danced around. He needed to learn that death is worthy of grief because it's final, for now. So we just sat on his bottom bunk and held each other tight.

Chase cried and shook and begged me for answers. He said, *It's not about Jacob, Mom. It's that everything we love is going die. How do we survive that?* And before I could answer, he said, *I know what you're going to say about heaven, Mom, but how do you **know** it's real? You **don't**. And I don't know if I can believe in it.*

I didn't offer many brilliant answers to my baby's brilliant questions. I was just grateful to be able to tell him truthfully that *Yes,* I believe that there is some sort of heaven, though I doubt it's like anything we've heard described. When he asked *how* I believed, I told him that I believe because I *have* to—because if I didn't believe, the terror that was gripping his heart, the terror of losing the people I love forever, would overtake me and I'd have no joy or hope and I'd die inside. I told him that I believe because I have no other choice, because I was made to believe, because if I didn't believe in life after death I wouldn't be able to live life before death. I'd panic and then freeze. When he asked me what I believed heaven was like, I told him that I believe heaven is a place where everyone loves each other perfectly.

When he asked me, *Why, Mom? Why does God send us here, where things hurt so much? Why does he make us love things that he knows we're going to lose?* I told him that we don't love people and animals because we will have them forever; we love them because loving them changes us, makes us better, healthier, kinder, realer. Loving people and animals makes us stronger in the right ways and weaker in the right ways. Even if animals and people leave, even if they die, they leave us *better*. So we keep loving, even though we might lose, because loving teaches us and changes us. And that's what we're here to do. God sends us here to learn how to be better lovers, and to learn how to be loved, so we'll be prepared for heaven.

When I finished this part, Chase looked right into my eyes. His tears cleared for a moment and he said, "Yes. I can believe that part. That sounds right. I believe that."

After a few more minutes, Tish walked into Chase's room, her eyes still red and her lips still quivering. She climbed onto the bunk and wedged herself between Chase and me. Craig and Amma followed her in and lay down on the floor together. Tish said softly, "I want Jacob to come back to life." Chase lifted his head toward Tish and with glistening eyes, he said, "Well, he won't come back to life here, but he will in heaven. So it's not all sad, Tish." Then he stopped crying. Sometimes the only way to transcend grief is to help someone littler transcend hers.

I stepped gratefully through the door of hope that Chase had opened for us. I had been waiting for his permission, because the one closest to the departed has to be the first to step from despair to hope. Nobody else is allowed to jump ahead and shove open the door. That's the rule.

I said, "Hey, guys, do you think in heaven, Jacob won't be a fighting fish anymore? Maybe in heaven he'll be a peaceful fish and finally get to swim around with his buddies and play."

Chase's eyes still glistened while a tiny smile emerged like a hesitant rainbow. This might be his best look. And it is my favorite moment in life. When you realize, *Wow, this is bad. Really, really bad. But we're still here. We're gonna make it through. Not over or under or around, but through. And look, we're even going to smile again.*

Tish's tears stopped, but her head remained resolutely in my lap. The five of us sat quietly for a little while, petting each other. Then we planned a proper send-off for Jacob in the backyard the following morning. We'd color some pictures for him and read a prayer and a poem or two. Then Chase ended our wake by dismissing himself to hold his guinea pig, Romeo. It was his wake to end.

Transcendentalist

One November morning, my children were very, very bad—due to the Halloween candy sugar-high, obviously. After lunch, I insisted that their teeth were going to fall out and they could have no more candy ever, ever, ever. The problem is that I love candy. So I told them not to eat it and I hid the stash, and then throughout the day, *I* ate it. Later, as I was putting the clothes in the dryer, I found a pack of mini-Twizzlers in Chase's pocket. They were all gummy and jacked up from going through the wash, but this was not a strong deterrent. Because: Twizzlers! I ripped the package open and started chewing. *Joy.*

But then I bit down on something hard. Weird. I examined the messy gob and found a tooth in it. A TOOTH. Upon second glance, I realized it was one of my crowns. I was terrified. It was like having one of those dreams in which your teeth are falling out and you wake up so relieved it was just a dream except that my teeth were actually falling out. No waking up. Tish walked in and I showed her the tooth, and she started crying. I thought she was worried about me, but no. Not Tish.

Tish: What's that red stuff in that tooth? Are you eating candy without me????

Me: Yes, Tish. I was.

Tish: And your tooth fell out???

Me: Yep. I *told* you.

Tish: Uh-oh. We better ask Google what we should do.

Google is her third parent. Actually, it may be her first parent. So I ran to the computer and entered: What do I do if my crown falls out? Got some good info. Thank you, Mama Google.

I took Mama Google's advice and made an appointment to get the crown replaced. I made sure to schedule it during the day so I could get a sitter and avoid telling Craig about the debacle. I cannot talk to my husband about the dentist. Craig is a total dental goody-goody. He goes to the dentist every six months, on the dot, and he flosses every day. Twice a day, often. I do not floss. I have no idea why not. I can do hard things, but not this easy thing. I'm too tired. This makes Craig insane. He leaves dental floss by my toothbrush every night. He sends me annoying links about gum disease. He buys me fresh toothbrushes every few months. He panics every time I open a package with my teeth. It's exhausting.

When I say that Craig is the poster boy for dental hygiene, I mean it literally. There is a mammoth poster of him on the wall at our local dentist, smiling his huge lily-white, healthy gummed smile, mocking all of us terrified, sweating, miserable anti-dentites. The entire dental staff adores Craig, and he loves them right back. He gushes about them while I glare at him. When he visits, they treat him like their son who's just come home from college. They ooh and aah. When I visit, they just eeewww. They raise their eyebrows. They look at my bleeding gums and then shoot each other glances and say to me, "You're not flossing. You're still not flossing." And then they pull out the dental floss and offer me a lesson. Every time, another flossing lesson. Like I'm five. And the thing is that I have to listen and pay attention and act like it's the first time I've ever seen someone floss because my only other alternative is to say, "JESUS—I KNOW how to floss, I JUST CHOOSE NOT TO." Which seems worse. So like an idiot, I watch them carefully and I say, "Ooooh, I see. That's how it's done. I use the floss on my teeth. Aaah . . . That's where I went wrong. I was using it on my elbow . . . I see now. Aha. Yes. I see. Looks fun!" It is always so uncomfortable and infuriating and humiliating that when I leave, I vow to floss every day. But then I don't. Because I get tired again.

The kids' dental appointments are different. I really like taking the kids to the dentist. We go to a dentist who's discovered that if you turn the office into an amusement park with movie screens and air hockey tables and video games kids will actually WANT to get cavities and JACKPOT! I'll take it, though. It's like Disneyland minus the walking around plus a Keurig machine and up-to-date *People* magazines.

As a bonus, I feel like a responsible grown-up at the kids' dentist. What kind of mom remembers to bring all three of her kids to the dentist? An amazing one, that's what kind. And so I walk around that office feeling very fancy and efficient. I always wear a cardigan to the kids' dental appointments. I only own one cardigan, because I'm not really the cardigan type. But on dentist day, I sure am. Nothing says responsible and OBVIOUSLY I'VE NEVER SPENT TIME IN JAIL DON'T BE RIDICULOUS like a cardigan does.

The sugar-free icing on the cake is that Craig the dental nerd makes our kids brush and floss twice a day, so they always get perfect dental reports. And since I'm the one who takes them to their appointments, the dentist thinks I'm the responsible dental parent and always congratulates me. Hah!

I once took the kids to a hotel without Craig, and at bedtime I had to tell the three of them that I forgot all of their toothbrushes. They turned WHITE (to be clear, my kids are half

Asian, so they're usually brown). These children were horrified. When I went into the bathroom to wash up, Tish found my cell phone, hid in the corner, and CALLED CRAIG TO RAT ME OUT. I heard her whispering furtively, "Daddy—Mommy said to go to bed without brushing our TEETH. What should we do, Daddy?" I ran out of the bathroom and yelled, "TISH! OH MY GOD," and Tish whispered back into the phone, "I have to go, Daddy, 'cause now Mommy's screaming bad words at me."

The next day when we got home, Craig started to say, "What the . . ." but I said DON'T EVEN. And he didn't even.

The point is, I'm bad at teeth cleaning, but I do use tooth whitener religiously. So when I get the kids' glowing teeth reports, I flash the hygienists my glowing smile and nobody's the wiser. In short, I get to be somebody else for a while—a dental nerd in a cardigan with perfectly groomed children—and I really enjoy playing that role for an hour or two. On dental mornings I become my own character foil.

One morning the kids had appointments scheduled, so I pulled on my cardigan, and we piled into the van. Unfortunately, I realized a few seconds later that I had forgotten to feed them breakfast. Usually I keep a dozen energy bars in the car for moments such as these, but on this day, I looked into the glove compartment and realized there was only one bar left. And I was starving. So obviously I told the kids there were no bars left and Amma was MAD, but what else is new? At the light, I turned up the music so they couldn't hear the wrapper, and I scarfed down that bad boy.

We arrived at dental Disneyland, and I sat in my comfy seat, reading my *People* magazine in my cardigan while the kids played air hockey. I tried to sit up very straight because I feel like responsible dental-cardigany people should have good posture. But I couldn't relax because Amma was being really loud. Too loud. So I called her over and whispered to her sweet little face, "You. must.lower.your.voice."

She pulled away dramatically and glared at me. Her face looked shocked. She pointed her chubby little finger right in my face and YELLED, "MOMMY! YOU SMELL LIKE A BAR! YOU SMELL LIKE A BAR, MOMMY!!! WHAT DID YOU DO, MOMMY?" Then she lay down on the floor and cried. She cried like—I don't know—like a child who'd been betrayed. Like a child who maybe just learned that her mama fell off the wagon. Like a child from that intervention show. Exactly like that.

Okay. So the waiting room was very crowded, and all of sudden the noise just stopped. All the other cardigany moms looked up from their parenting magazines and right at me. They couldn't look away, although I'm sure they really wish they could have.

That was when I remembered that I had a 1 billion ounce transparent water bottle with me, filled to the rim with BEET JUICE. This is the sort of thing one recovering from Lyme disease has to drink in the morning. But unfortunately, all I could consider was how incredibly much it looked like a forty-ounce bloody mary.

Briefly, I thought about standing up and making an announcement:

AHEM! Listen, you guys. This is just a misunderstanding. This is actually really funny. Funnier than you can even imagine! Ironic, even. Because, you see, I'm NOT drunk this morning, but I actually WAS, for like twenty years! But now I drink BEET JUICE. This is BEET JUICE. And this crying, kicking one— she's talking about ENERGY BARS. I smell like ENERGY bars. Isn't that hilarious? I'm not drunk. Swearsies.

No. One can't make an announcement like this. I decided that pretty quickly. It hit me that that the best thing I could do was just ACT SOBER.

Now the single best way to appear wasted when you are not wasted is to TRY HARD NOT TO ACT WASTED. Go ahead: try to act sober when you really ARE sober but also paranoid that people think you're drunk. It's impossible. You end up trying so hard to walk straight that you teeter. You try so hard to enunciate clearly that you sound like a robotic idiot. In short, the harder you try to look sober, the more you forget what sober looks like or even feels like, and the drunker you appear to be. THAT is what happened to me. I dropped my magazine. I tripped. I spilled my beet juice on my one and only cardigan. Cardigan! HA! Clearly a sham. Might as well have worn my Mötley Crüe shirt with yoga pants and called it a day.

We made it through the appointments. I stared in my rearview mirror the whole ride home CERTAIN that the dental office had called a police escort. I didn't see any, but still, I demanded the kids stay silent the whole way home so I could CONCEN-TRATE ON DRIVING SOBER.

I swerved. I failed to obey the minimum speed and then the maximum. I forgot to use my blinker. We finally made it home, exhausted and frenzied. I immediately went to find the candy stash.

Officer Superhero

It's December 23 and I'm at Target with Tish and Amma. We've made it through the shopping part and we're in the checkout line. I can see the Promised Land, which is: *We're Done Shopping, Let's Go Back Home.*

I watch Amma notice a pack of Gummi Worms. Her eyes widen. I brace for chaos. She grabs the worms, shows them to me with tears in her eyes, and says, **"I need dese worms!"** I say, "Yep. That's the magic Target spell. It makes me think I need all this junk, too. The Target spell is why you're not going to college, baby. No Gummi Worms. Put them down."

There is no way to convey the drama that was unleashed on poor unsuspecting Target immediately following the word *down*.

Amma threw herself onto the filthy floor and screamed like a person who maybe just found out that her entire family died. Amma's particular tantrum style is that she chooses one phrase to repeat 7 million times at 7 million decibels until everyone around her seriously considers homicide or suicide. On this day, she chose, "I SO *HUNGWY*! I SO *FIRSTY*!" (*SKULL-SPLITTING SCREAM.*) "I SO *HUNGWY*! I SO *FIRSTY*!" (*SKULL-SPLITTING SCREAM.*)

This was a long, crowded line. And every time the line scootched up, I had to grab Amma's hood and drag her forward a few feet while she kicked and screamed, like I do with my luggage in the security lines at the airport. And then Tish started crying because it was all so ridiculous. So I gritted my teeth and made my scariest face at Tish and growled *STOP* at her like some kind of movie monster, but this sort of thing does not tend to calm down a child. So she cried harder. People started moving away from us, and shoppers were actually stopping by our aisle to stare. I was sweating like I was in a sauna, and wishing the "It's the Most Wonderful Time of the Year" song that was on repeat would just *end. With the kids jinglebelling and everyone telling you, be of good cheer!* Right. My experience **exactly.**

Up until this point, I had kept my head down, but it seemed time to offer my best beleaguered, apologetic, *what are you gonna do?* looks to the other shoppers, in hopes of receiving some sympathetic looks in return.

But when I finally looked up, I realized with mounting discomfort that there weren't going to be any sympathetic looks. *Everyone* was staring at me. *Every. One.* One elderly couple looked so disturbed that the grandmother had her hand over her mouth and was holding tight to her husband's arm. At first it appeared to be an effort to shield herself from my rabid animals. I thought, *I hear ya lady, they scare me too.* But then I realized that she wasn't looking disapprovingly at *them;* she was looking disapprovingly at *me.* I locked eyes with her, and without subtlety, she looked down at my clothes, then to my cart, and then away.

So I did the same thing. Down at myself, then to the cart. *Ooooooooohhhh,* I thought. *Shoot.*

My Lyme was back, and I'd been sick for a little while. The day before had been a bad Lymie day, and so was the day before that, so I may have forgotten to shower or brush my hair. For forty-eight hours. And also, when I looked down I noticed that I still had on my pajama top. Which apparently I had *tucked in* to my ripped jeans. Like seventh grade. I looked bad. Not *a little* bad—*offensively, aggressively* bad. Also, here is what was in my cart: *six large bottles of wine and curtain rods*. It looked like I planned to create a wine bong. Which wouldn't have been so bad if my smallest child would have stopped screaming: *"I SO HUNGWY, I SO FIRSTY!"*

And since I was so tired and in such a state of self-pity, I couldn't even bring myself to *feign* sympathy toward my starving, parched child on the floor. Because I *wasn't* sympathetic, not even a little bit. I *definitely* remembered feeding her the previous day. Faker.

I resigned myself to suffer through. I stopped trying to help the girls at all. Just left Amma there on the floor screaming and Tish beside her crying and prayed the line would move faster. I am certain that even the atheists in that line were praying it would move faster.

All of a sudden, a uniformed police officer started walking toward us. At first I was alarmed and defensive. But as he stopped in front of me, he smiled warmly and winked.

He looked down at the girls and said, *"May I?"*

I was not sure what he was asking exactly, but I allowed myself to hope that he would arrest them and take them away. So I nodded.

The police officer patted Amma on the head gently. She looked up at him and stopped mid-scream. She stood up. Tish fell silent and grabbed Amma's hand. All of a sudden they became a pair of grubby little soldiers. At attention, eyes shining, terrified.

The officer said, *"Hello, girls. Have you two ever heard of 'disturbing the peace'?"*

They shook their little heads *no*.

He smiled and continued, *"Well, that means that your mama*

and all of these people are trying to shop in peace, and you are disturbing them, and you're not allowed to. Can you try to be more peaceful?"

They nodded their little heads yes.

The officer stood back up and smiled at me. I tried really hard to show my gratitude by smiling back.

I noticed that the girls grabbed each other in a bear hug and held on for dear life. They had lived to die another day.

He said, *"Being a parent. It's a tough gig sometimes."*

For some reason, I was suddenly desperate to be perceived by him as something other than a struggling mom, so I blurted out, "I'm also a writer."

He looked genuinely interested and said, *"Really? What do you write?"*

"Lots of things. Mostly a blog."

"What's it about?"

"Parenting, I guess."

His eyes twinkled, and he grinned and said teasingly, *"Oh. Does anybody read it?"*

And I said, "A few. Mostly for laughs, though. Not for, well, advice. Obviously."

I miraculously found the energy and ability and space and breath to giggle.

And my officer smiled and said the following:

"You know, my wife and I raised six kids, and I think that's actually the only parenting advice worth a damn. Just try to keep laughing. Try to keep laughing. It's good advice. You're doing good, Mom."

Then he tipped his hat to me and my girls, and walked away.

In the end, only kindness matters. Thank you, Officer Superhero. Merry Christmas.

The girls were silent until halfway home from Target when Tish announced loudly, *"I can't believe we almost went to jail. We better not tell Daddy."*

And I said, "No way. We *have* to tell him. What if we don't and then he sees the report on the news tonight?"

Big eyes. More silence.

Joy to the World.

On Gifts and Talents

I've been thinking about my parent friends for whom the start of the school year is a difficult time, because the classroom has proven to be a tough place for their child to display his particular brand of genius.

For these precious mamas, starting school means revisiting old worries and facing new ones. It means tears and tense phone calls and scary conferences and comparisons and lots of fear and anger and suspicion and *Oh My God, Is He All Right? And What Are We Doing Wrong?*

I'd like to talk to you about your brilliant children.

Listen.

Every child is gifted and talented. Every single one. *I know* this to be true. Every single child is gifted and talented in a particular area. Every single one also has particular challenges. For some kids, the classroom setting is the place where their genius is hardest to see and their challenges are easiest to see. And since they spend so much time in the classroom, that's a tough break for these little guys. But if we are patient and calm and we wear our perspectacles and we keep believing, we will eventually see the specific magic of each child.

Like my student who was severely dyslexic and also could've won a comedy contest at age seven. One time he was waiting at the water fountain and said, "Lord, Miss Doyle. I been waitin' in this line since I was *six*." *The boy was a genius.*

Like my precious one who couldn't walk or speak because of his severe cerebral palsy, but whose smile while completing his grueling physical therapy inspired the rest of my class to call him the "bravest." *Genius, that kid.*

Like my little man with autism, who couldn't have hurt another living being if somebody paid him to. He was the most gentle soul I've ever known. And he loved animals like they were a gift made just for him by God. Which, of course, they were. But nobody in our class knew that except him. *Undeniable Genius.*

Like my third grader who read like a kindergartner and couldn't add yet. But one day I stood behind her at recess, where she played all alone, and heard her singing to herself. That was the day I discovered her gift. It was also the day that *she* discovered her gift, because I freaked out. And I marched her over to the rest of the teachers and made her sing for them. And when we came in from recess, I announced to my class that we had a *rock star* in our midst. And she quietly beamed. And she sang all the time after that. *All the time.* Actually, it was a little much. But we let it slide because *you don't mess with artistic genius.*

Or the little man in one of Chase's classes who was always getting in trouble. Every day, *getting in trouble*. And Chase came home one day and said, "I think he's not listening because he's always making pictures in his head. He's the best drawer I've ever seen. He's going to be famous, I bet." Chase was right. I've seen this kid's work. *Genius.*

Or my little one who was gifted in the classroom-learning way and was miles ahead of the other kids in every single subject. But she had challenges being kind and humble about her particular strengths, so she had trouble making friends. Sometimes it's *tough to be a genius.*

Every single child is gifted. And every child has challenges. It's just that in the educational system, some gifts and challenges are harder to see. And teachers are working on this problem. Lots of schools are trying to find ways to make all children's gifts visible and celebrated. And as parents, we can help. We can help our kids who struggle in school believe that they're okay. It's just that there's only one way to help them. And it's hard.

We have to *actually believe* that our kids are okay.

I know. Tough. But it *can* be done. We can start believing by erasing the idea that education is a race. It's not. Education is like *Christmas.* We're all just opening our gifts, one at a time. And it is a fact that each and every child has a bright shiny present with her name on it, waiting there underneath the tree. God wrapped it up, and he'll let us know when it's time to unwrap it. In the meantime, we must believe that our children are okay. Every last one of them. The straight-A ones and the ones with autism and the naughty ones and the chunky ones and the shy ones and the loud ones and the *so-far-behind* ones.

Because here's what I believe: a child can survive a teacher or other children accidentally suggesting that he's not okay, as long as when he comes home, he looks at his mama and knows by her face that he *really is okay.* Because that's all they're asking, isn't it?

Mama, am I okay?

In the end, a child will call the rest of the world liars and believe his mama.

So when he asks us with his eyes and heart if he's okay, let's tell him:

Yes, baby. You are okay. You are more than okay. You are my dream come true. You are everything I've ever wanted, and I wouldn't trade one you for a **million** anybody elses. *This part of life, this school part, might be hard for you. But that's okay, because it's just one part of life. And because we can do hard things, together. We are a team. And I am so grateful to be on your team.*

And then, before we dive into "helping," let's just eat some cookies together and talk about other things. There are so many other things to talk about, really.

Let's be Atticus Finch in *To Kill a Mockingbird*. Atticus's children, Scout and Jem, carefully watch their father's behavior as the house next door to theirs burns to the ground. As the fire creeps closer and closer to the Finches' home, Atticus appears so calm that Scout and Jem finally decide that "it ain't time to worry yet."

We need to be Atticus. *Hands in our pockets. Calm. Believing.* So that our children will look at us and even with a fire raging in front of them, they'll say, "Huh. Guess it's not time to worry yet."

Then we'll watch carefully. We'll just *watch and wait and believe* until God nods and says, "It's time. Tear open that gift, Mama."

And we'll get to say our Mama FAVE. *Told you so. Told you so, World.*

Mommy Do-Little

I have a teeny, tiny, furry problem.

One August morning, Craig asked if he could bring his parents' toy poodle to our house for a few days. I said yes, but only for the sake of the children.

I don't dig animals. I allow Chase to watch *Animal Planet* when I'm not in the room, but other than that, I keep my distance. All the licking and sniffing and scales and feathers and fur . . . I mean, really. Life is messy enough already.

Speaking of messy, I recently quit parenting. I do not parent in August. August parenting is not a good look for me. It's hotter than hell, and the children and I have already had a *whole lot* of togetherness. Don't get me wrong, summer is grand, and I really enjoy all the lack of structure and living in the moment and so on and so forth. Truly. Just lovely. But no more. I refuse to enjoy another moment until the moments change significantly. So at August's family meeting, I smiled pretty and announced to the children that I was officially done with the following:

1. Smiling when you people spill things. I am *past* the mommy point of no return. Which means that I can no longer pretend that I'm not mad at you when you spill your cereal, water, or entire dinner plate fifteen seconds after I put it in front of you. I know I've been acting calm

165

and saying, "It's okay, sweetie," through clenched teeth for a few years now. That's all over. It's not okay, actually. If you spill, expect the wrath. Prepare for it, take a deep breath, 'cause it's a-comin'. Oh yes, I know *it was an accident, Mom!* and I'm sure your future therapist will be happy to talk to you about how this injustice made you feel. Please know that I have forgiven myself unequivocally for my unfairness, random rage, and unforgiveness, and I can only hope that this will bring you comfort.

2. Feigning fascination with stories that have *absolutely no point* and are punctuated by excruciating pauses of approximately three minutes after each and every word. Your stories start after breakfast, and by the time you are done, it's time for me to prepare lunch. And they're not good. They are really **NOT good** stories. I really don't even understand what you're *saying.* I plan to suggest that your teachers skip geography this fall and instead teach some storytelling skills so that your audience is not forced to smile manically at you while internally twitching and fantasizing about how to suffocate herself. Every time you say "Mom . . . listen," I feel as powerless and panicked as an unarmed hostage. For the remainder of the summer, I am going to carry a buzzer around with me. If you begin a story and it does not end within two minutes, I am going to buzz you very loudly and walk away.

3. Putting you to bed forty different times each night. Every bedtime is like a twisted game of Whack-A-Mole. If you come out of that room, prepare to get Whacked.

4. Also, no more "reading to me" at bedtime. Let's see. It takes you six minutes to sound out each word, so if your book is one hundred words, well, I don't specialize in math, but

I'm pretty sure we will be "reading" that book until I **die**. And I can't help but notice that the ONLY TIME YOU CARE THIS MUCH ABOUT *READING IT YOUR-SELF* IS AT BEDTIME. When you can again hold me hostage and stay up six minutes later with every sounded-out word. And so while I'm supposed to be thinking sweet prideful thoughts about your reading and smelling your freshly washed hair, all I can think is: *OH MY GOD. I AM GOING TO DIE. YOU SUCK AT READING.* From now on: Reading is for SCHOOL ONLY. If this means you'll go back to school in September unable to keep up with your classmates, so be it. A little humility never hurt anybody. NO MORE READING.

5. Refereeing. I will no longer intervene to save you. So as my wise friend tells her children, *if you are going to fight, be prepared to fight to the death.*

6. Cooking, cleaning, playing, teaching, smiling . . . talking, even, really. If you need parental assistance, call Bubba and Tisha instead. Number's on the fridge. I'll be in my room. Please knock *only after* you observe pumpkins and football jerseys and piles of leaves and you have enrolled yourself in several after-school activities.

Love you forever.

Anyway, Craig suggested poodle sitting the day after I'd submitted my mommy resignation, and I thought, *Jackpot.* I figured the kids could play with the dog for four days, and it'd seem like a family activity without my actually having to organize any family activities. My personal goal for the dog's visit was to disguise my disgust for her as effectively as possible. Then she arrived.

Oh My God. I loved her. I decided I needed my own, exactly *now*.

So I wrote on Facebook that I needed advice "for a friend" who was considering dog adoption. I couldn't admit that the friend was actually *me* because I didn't want anyone trying to talk some sense into me.

In response to my request, my old friend Mandy suggested that "my friend" consider adopting a rescue dog. Mandy spends most of her time and heart taking care of homeless doggies. After I admitted that "my friend" was me, Mandy asked specifics about what kind of dog we were looking for. I told her that I wanted a *near-comatose dog*. I wanted a *semi-stoned* dog. I wanted a dog that liked the couch as much as I do. She promised to keep her eyes open as she visited the local shelters.

Eventually, Mandy e-mailed me and said, "I may have found your dog. Just did a behavior evaluation on a stray Lhasa Apso that was the chillest, most gentle dog I've ever seen. He's white, about five years old, and he's got a Brando-like underbite that makes him so ugly he's cute."

When I read the ugly thing, I knew he was mine. With the exception of husbands, I always choose the ugly one. Craig won't let me choose our Halloween pumpkins or Christmas trees. When I told Craig that Mandy found our dog, he said, "NO, Glennon. I am **not** *feeling* a dog right now. No. **No way.**"

I looked at him for a minute and smiled.

He paused and said, "Yeah. I'm done. When can we meet him?"

So the next day we told the kids we were going to visit some homeless doggies and love on them for a while. When we arrived, the shelter people led us through a huge room of kennels. Every single dog was barking like mad. It was a little chaotic and intimidating. Amma was scared. And by Amma, I mean me.

But then we got to the very end of the row of kennels, and in the very last cage, this little fluffy guy quietly walked toward us, peeked his head out, wagged his tail, and licked Chase's hand. No barking, no jumping, just wagging and kisses. Craig later said that Theo seemed to be saying, "*Well . . .* there you are. I *knew* you'd come."

We named him Theo because Mandy's maiden name was Theobald, and since she found him for us, Theo seemed right. We later found out that Theo means "gift from God."

The next day the shelter called us and said that our doggie was *very close* to becoming our doggie, and that we could pick him up as soon as they sent him to be groomed and neutered. They explained that since Theo was a stray, he was quite matted and dirty and needed to be *freshened up*.

I called Craig and said: "**Husband!** We have a problem. *No way* are they grooming him before he comes home." Craig paused and said, *"Why, honey?"* (A little too wearily, I thought.)

I said, *"Because!* I don't want him to think that he has to be *all cleaned up and pretty* in order for us to want him! No way. He comes home *just as he is. We'll* clean him up. I love him all jacked up. *He comes home all jacked up."*

Craig: *I can't say I really understand that.*

Me: Well, that's fine because I understand it enough for both of us.

(silence)

Sister beeps in on call waiting

Me: Gotta go, husband, Sister is calling.

Husband: *(sigh of relief)*

Me: **Sister!** They want to groom Theo before he comes home, and this is unacceptable!

Sister: *Why, Sister?*

Me: Because I don't want him to feel like we didn't love him enough *as he is* to bring him home.

Sister: *Oooooookay. Let me try to understand. You . . . don't . . . want . . . him . . . to . . . feel . . . like . . . you . . . didn't . . . **love** . . . him . . . enough.*

Me: *Why* do people always repeat what I say verrrrrrrrrrry slowly and make it sound all crazy???

Sister: It doesn't sound crazy because it's being repeated slowly, Sister. *That's not the reason.* The things you say sound crazy *before* they're repeated. We are just hoping you'll *hear* the crazy if we repeat it back to you.

Me: Whatever. Listen, Amma's pretty now, but do you remember what she looked like when she was born? We didn't insist on a *make-over* before *she* came home.

Sister: (silence) *You are unreasonable, Sister.*

Me: (silence back) *Well.* Hm. *While we are on the subject of unreasonable,* Sister, I feel obliged to tell you that I find it *completely unreasonable* that you *continue to try to **reason*** with me after having known me for *THIRTY-FOUR YEARS.*

Sister: You have a point, Sister. Yes, you do. Go get your dog. We'll groom him later.

Me: 'Kay. *Thank you.* But I'm taking him back to the shelter next week so *they* can send him to get neutered. I don't want Theo to think *that part* was my idea. That's on *them.*

Sister: (Silence) *Fine, Sister.*

I went to pick him up at the shelter later that week. I was extremely nervous for the final interview, so I called one of my besties, Christy, because she fosters dogs and often facilitates interviews with potential families. When she answered, I said, "Oh my God I'm on my way for my final interview and what if they ask if I take antidepressants and what if they read my blog and what if they ask me if I have ever been to jail or inhaled and just, *oh my God.*"

And Christy said, "**Glen.** Breathe deep. This is not like adopting a person. Just don't mention Michael Vick, and you'll be fine."

So I took a deep breath and walked into the shelter. I began my interview with a lovely dog trainer named Feather, and as soon as she started talking, I knew I'd be okay. I mean, really—anyone who dedicates her life to helping animals or young children is okay in my book. It seems to me that these are two of the only vocations for which there can be no other motive than gentleness and love. Because when you are working with animals or children, there are usually no grown-ups around to give you kudos or respect or much money. It's just you and the powerless ones and God.

So, as you would expect, Feather was good to me. And halfway through the interview, Sister showed up at the shelter. Because Sister *always* shows up. And now since she is John's, he's gotta show up too. He doesn't mind too much because he's a natural shower-upper.

Sister was so excited she looked like she might pee. A new nephew, you know. The previous night she had arrived at my house with a doggie *car seat* and a zebra-striped doggie bed and thirty-dollar Bed Head strawberry banana doggie *detangler spray.* I know. But that's Sister. When they brought my doggie out, Sister held him first.

When Tish was born, Sister was the first one of us to touch her. She held Tish's hand first. Before me, before Craig. It's natural for us. My babies are her babies.

And then Sister handed me my doggy, and we left together. Just me and him. He sat in my lap the entire ride home. He was a little shaky, but that was okay, because so was I. I cried a lot. Because after years of praying and wishing and hoping I would get to adopt, God *finally* let me.

When we got home, Craig was waiting on the floor in the foyer and Theo walked straight over to him and lay down in his lap—belly up, ready to soak up some love. The next morning we let Theo wake up each child, one at a time. The kids didn't know he had come home the previous night, so when they woke up to their very own doggy licking their cheeks, well . . . it was a good morning.

I don't know what this life is doing to me with all these love experiments, but I think one of these days I am just going to *melt* into this beautiful world.

The Golden Coin

A friend recently asked me this question:

How can we give our children the confidence they need to survive on earth and still encourage the humility that is pleasing to God?

My little brain's been flipping this over and over like a pancake that won't cook through. But I haven't considered it in terms of parenting. Usually when someone asks me a question about parenting, I switch it into a question about grown-ups. *How do I encourage my child to be kinder to others?* becomes, *How do I become kinder to others?* After reading the sixteenth parenting book that contradicted the first fifteen, I quit trying to become a better parent and decided to try becoming a better person.

We usually think of confidence and humility as character traits. She's so *confident*. He's so *humble*. But these character traits are easy to fake. Insecure people hide it by boasting. Prideful people hide behind false humility. It seems the more insecure a person is, the more likely she is to *behave confidently*. And vice versa. Tricky.

Then there are people like me who just get the two constantly mixed up. Like when I write an essay about humility and then spend the rest of the day wondering whether it might actually be the best humility essay ever written by anyone in the history of the world. The character trait I am most proud of is my humility.

I am so humble, it's not even funny. Seriously, just don't try to out-humble me. I will *wreck* your teeny little humility with my HUGE HUMILITY.

Even though I feel like a lost cause in regard to this confidence/humility issue, I do think it's an important thing to explore. Because if we are humble without confidence, we miss the opportunity to become what we want to be when we grow up. And if we are confident without humility, we miss out on becoming *who* we want to be when we grow up.

I think about it all the time in terms of my writing. Spilling myself out like this, is it an act of humility or confidence? I share my faults and flaws, which seems humble—but isn't the fact that I assume that others will *care enough to read* and maybe even find my flaws *charming* betray the confidence behind my humility? Writing, painting, acting, creating, living out loud: Are they acts of humility or confidence?

Yes. They're both. That's what I've decided. Confidence and humility are two sides of the same coin. They are character traits that stem from the two beliefs I hold most dear. I think most of our character traits are simply manifestations of what we believe to be true.

I am *confident* because I believe that I am a child of God. I am *humble* because I believe that everyone else is too.

They go hand in hand. They've got to.

If I am humble but lack confidence, it is because I haven't accepted that there is a divine spark inside me. It means that I don't believe in the miracle that I was made by God for a purpose all my own, and so I am worthy of the space that I occupy on this earth. And that as a child of God, no one deserves more respect, joy, or peace than I. As a child of God, I have the right to speak, to feel, to think, and to believe what I believe. Those dreams in my heart, those ideas in my head, they are real and they have a divine origin, and so they are worth exploring. *Just because I am a child of God*. And thankfully, there is nothing I can add to that title to make it more impressive. There is also nothing I can do to lose that title. I am confident not because I am pretty or smart or athletic or talented or kind. Those things change and can be given and taken. I am confident simply because I am a child of God.

That is why I am confident enough to write honestly. Not because I am a good writer. There will always be somebody better. I rely on the belief that I am a child of God, and as such, I have right to speak my mind with love. This writing thing, it's one of my dreams. And I act on my dreams because I believe that God is not just *with* me but *in* me. I believe that he is the creator of my dreams. So it follows that when I act on them, magical things will happen. How could they not? Being a child of God is a free pass to be brave and bold and take great risks and spin around in circles with joy. If and when I fall, who cares? He will always be there to pick me up. That's his **job**. He's my Father. So if I seem noncompetitive, if I seem as if I don't care if I'm the "best" parent or housekeeper or dresser or whathaveyou, it's not because I don't care about being important. It's because I believe I am the most important thing on earth. Why would I care about competing in any other category when I am already a child of God? Why would I argue over a penny when I have already won the lottery?

And.

If I am confident but not humble, it is because I have not fully accepted that *everyone* has won the lottery. Because everyone has the same amount of God in her. If I am in the habit of turning my back on others, it is because I haven't learned that

God approaches us in the disguise of other people. If I am confident but not humble, my mind is closed. If my mind if closed, my heart is closed. A closed heart is so sad. It is the end. A heart cannot grow any larger if it decides to let no more God in. There is always room for more. A heart expands exactly as much as her owner allows.

Humility is how I survive praise and criticism of my writing, ideas, and beliefs. Because I remember that neither praise nor criticism is really about me. We are all just trying to find the truth. So I try to see different points of view not as reasons to step back further into my corner, but as opportunites to take baby steps toward the middle of the ring—if for no other reason than to see my opponent a little closer. That perspective change is usually all it takes to remember that I *have* no opponents other than my pride.

I am a child of God, and so is everyone else. We are all on the same side. And so in each new person, I see an invitation to know a new side of God. There are as many sides of him as there are people walking the earth. I think that's why he keeps making people. He's not done telling us about himself yet. So I remember that each person I meet or hear from, even if she's not yet treating me the way I'd like to be treated, is the most important thing on earth. There is no hierarchy of importance, of brilliance. We are each *infinity important. More brilliant than the sun.* Because each of us is a child of God. So we *better recognize.*

Those are the two sides of the golden coin I'd like each of my children to keep in her pocket forever:

Be confident because you are a child of God. Be humble because everyone else is too.

Closer to Fine

Lately I've been exploring the disciplines that help me fill up and remain calm. Most of these techniques are proactive things I do *before I am upset* to remind myself that the world and I are all right. These things are good, and they help me maintain a peaceful heart to some extent. But I live with three small children, and I am convinced that they meet early in the morning to plan the most effective way to take me down. So the fact is that my peace is not going to be consistently maintained, no matter how much reading, writing, praying, or yoga I do. Because there are *very* strong-willed forces working against me.

Allow me to offer a specific example. The other night at dinner, Craig and I demanded that the kids clean their plates even though dinner was, admittedly, gross. One nanosecond before this suggestion was made, we were laughing, talking about Daddy's day at work, planning our upcoming weekend, and generally feeling like a lovely, well-adjusted family. Then—*ambushed by ourselves again*—there was crying, screaming, heads banging on tables. Immediate anarchy. Instant chaos.

I know that there are mothers who can roll with these scenarios. When kids tantrum, their facial expressions don't change. Their weary smiles suggest: "Oh, well, kids will be kids," and they calmly do whatever needs to be done to diffuse the situation. This approach is not my first instinct. My first instinct is to *freak out*.

My first instinct is to remember that yes, this chaos is proof that I have ruined my life and the lives of everyone in my home and that we are a disaster of a family and that no mother, in the entire history of mothers, has ever been forced to endure the drama, decibels, and general suffering of this moment. My instinct is to tear my clothes and throw myself on the floor and bawl and cry out worthless declarations like, "I can't TAKE this anymore!" My first instinct is to allow my anxiety and angst to pour out like gasoline on a raging fire and indulge in a full-on mommy meltdown.

This, Craig suggests, is not helpful.

So after a few years of parenting, it became clear that I needed a strategy to help me regain my peace *after I had already lost it*. Because I am going to lose it—frequently.

Enter Joan Didion. Ms. Didion is a serious writer. Every word she chooses is precise and perfect. In an essay called "Self-Respect," Ms. Didion offers the only strategy that has ever consistently helped me regain my mommy peace once I've lost it:

> It was once suggested to me that as an antidote to crying, I put my head in a paper bag. As it happens, there is a sound physiological reason, something to do with oxygen, for doing exactly that, but the psychological effect alone is incalculable. It is difficult in the extreme to continue fancying oneself Cathy in *Wuthering Heights* with one's head in a food fair bag. There is a similar case for all the small disciplines, unimportant in themselves; imagine maintaining any sort of swoon, commiserate or carnal, in a cold shower.

Yes, Ms. Didion, *yes*. It's the little things. It's the little disciplines that help us get through the day and regain peace. It's not necessarily a different career or parenting philosophy or neighborhood or husband that we need. Sometimes it's a deep breath, a glass of water, or a paper bag.

I now store paper bag hats on all three floors of my house. When my children start losing their minds, I put on my bag and breathe and hide. Tah-dah! Instant quiet time, oxygen, and a reminder that things are not necessarily as dramatic and horrible as my kids or jumpy head might suggest.

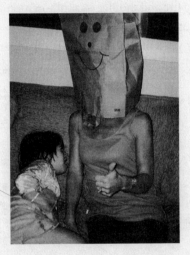

I draw smiley faces on my bags because I know that a large portion of my kids' mommy memories will include these bags, and I'd like them to be smiley memories. Also, I love how the smiley face makes me look content, even though inside I am scowling and hyperventilating and ruing the day I was born. I think the thumbs-up gesture really completes the effect. One piece of advice: if you decide to employ this strategy in your home, don't be tempted to cut out eye holes. I tried it once, and it ruins everything, because, well, eye holes mean you can still see the carnage, and the carnage can see your maniacal eyes.

No eye holes.

It's helpful to adopt "small disciplines" to remind one's self that life is much too important to be taken seriously.

HOLDING ON

On Crying and Pedaling

For Robert

I think what we're supposed to do down here is bring heaven to earth, and I saw that happen once. I experienced heaven on earth.

Years ago I participated in the AIDS ride as a fundraiser for AIDS research. Thousands of people raised money by pledging to ride their bicycles 280 miles from North Carolina to Washington, D.C. I was one of these thousands of people.

I was not the most likely candidate because I'd never done anything for charity, ever. Unless you count my spring break trip to an Indian reservation, but that was mostly to score peyote. Decreasing my candidacy further was my absolute hatred of physically hard things.

For example, trying to unlock a door that won't unlock has been known to leave me on my front step in a puddle of tears. God, I hate that. *The finding of the keys in my purse, the identifying of the correct key on the ring, the continuous turning of the key, the trying of the other keys, the dropping and retrieving of the keys, the juggling of bags and the whining kids and the sweat.* Life is so hard.

When Chase was eight, he started asking about "bad words." We decided to teach him all of them so they'd lose their allure, but I couldn't bring myself to say the F word out loud. Chase said, "It's okay. I think I know that one. It's the one you say when you can't get the door open, right?" Yes. *That one,* I said. *Don't say that one.*

Still, I agreed to do the AIDS ride. I'm not really sure why. I think I just wanted to be the sort of person who did those sorts of things. I think it's nice that God makes things magical even when we do them for lame reasons.

Most of the AIDS ride was hellish. Partly because I hadn't even *sat* on a bike since I was seven. I didn't even *have* a bike. Every time Dana asked me to train with her, I'd remain on the couch, close my eyes, and tell her I was training through "visualization." And although I did quit smoking and drinking as part of my preparation, I didn't *officially* start quitting until 2:00 a.m. on race day. This quitting method was less helpful than my drinking buddies had promised it would be.

Also, we rode our bikes *one hundred miles a day in ninety-five degree heat.* Our bottoms were so blistered and chapped that hourly we had to apply a product I'd have preferred never to discover called Butt Paste. At the end of each godforsaken day we rolled into "camp" and peeled off our soaking bike shorts to shower alongside other riders in a TRUCK. Honestly, I don't know if I've ever even *ridden* in a truck. Then we had to go to sleep in *a field.* It was like Woodstock with no music or drugs. Just pain. And there were terrifying Wizard of Oz–like storms at night and our tents leaked. So we lay in our own personal freezing ponds all night until we heard the fire alarm indicating it was time to ride again. Then we stood up and put helmets on our soaking heads and put our blistered, red, screaming butts back on our bike seats. I spent most of each day pedaling and crying. Crying and pedaling.

I wasn't the only one crying. I might have been the only one crying because of severe alcohol and nicotine withdrawal, but there were lots of tears. Tears from the sun's brutality and from witnessing the relentless resolve of other riders. Tears from passing families on the side of the road blowing bubbles and whistles and holding posters that said: *"YOU ARE A HERO."* That'll tear you up. It tore everybody up. You can't be called a hero when you're at your absolute weakest and not cry. You just can't. So you just cry and pedal.

Dana, Christy, and I lived together at the time, and Christy thought that we were nuts to be doing this AIDS ride. She was mostly annoyed because it cut so deeply into our trio's nightly wine and *Jeopardy!* ritual. Christy wasn't used to four days without us, so she drove to North Carolina and brought cookies to our camp site. Then she left and slept at a nice hotel. I begged her to take me along but she said *absolutely not* and promised that one day I'd thank her. It's been more than a decade since the ride, and I still haven't felt like thanking her. The next morning Christy found us again and drove beside Dana and me for half the day at two miles per hour, top down, smoking cigarettes and blasting "Eye of the Tiger" and "Livin' on a Prayer." Waving other cars around her for hours. Flipping them the bird when they honked at her. That's a friend.

There were rest stops along the way. Every few hours we'd pull over and find huge tents set up with volunteer medics scurrying around to bandage wounds, oxygenate wheezers, and take the sick to the hospital. I used these rests to inhale Power Bars, cry more, and pop zits. Sweating constantly causes acne, and this was distressing because there was a cute boy rider who was checking me out. So I kept a mini-mirror inside my bike pants even though it was *extremely uncomfortable,* and as soon as I hit each rest stop, I whipped it out and popped zits before the cute boy found me. Dana watched this routine in disgust. She'd gasp for air and pour bottled waters over her head and say: "Look at you. We're DYING and YOU'RE PRIMPING." And I'd say, "Well, THERE IS NO NEED TO DIE COVERED IN WHITE-HEADS NOW, *IS THERE?*" Got myself a post-ride date too. Yes. I did. Got me some digits on the AIDS ride.

Still. There were stretches that went on for hours. Just hours and hours of nothing but scorching sun and pain and regret, and all you could think about was taking back your decision to do this crazy thing. And then, in the midst of utter despair, you'd see *a mountain.* A mountain would appear on the horizon like a sick joke. Over and over. Mountain after mountain. Just when you'd think, *we have to be done.* There *can't* be another one. There'd be another one. And I'd get so angry. SO ANGRY. *WTF God???* Really, another freaking mountain now? Now when things are already SO DAMN BAD? Now, WHEN WE'RE TRYING TO DO SOMETHING NICE AND GOOD?

The problem was that there was no quitting. Even quitters like me couldn't quit. Nobody said it; we all just knew. Even so, I'd also know that I *just couldn't* take this next mountain. I just *couldn't.* My soul was willing, but my body was close to dead. So I approached one of the mountains, already defeated. And a thin, gray-skinned, baldish man on his own bike rode up beside me. The man had hollow cheeks and eyes that were set too far back, like caves. His leg muscles looked painted on. Just muscle and bone. So skinny and small, like a jockey with a vicious flu. I made confused eye contact with the grayish man and he put his hand on my back. He read my pain and said, "Just rest, I'll push you." And I cried and rested my legs and let myself be carried. I didn't understand how he was doing it, how he was pushing me up that hill, riding his bike and my bike, one hand on his handlebars and one hand on my back. But slowly, together, we made it to the top. And I squeaked out a thank-you, and he looked right at me with his cavey eyes and said: *thank YOU*. Then he turned away from me and rode back down the hill to carry another rider who couldn't carry himself. And I turned back to watch him go and saw that there were at least twenty of these angels—twenty men with hands on the backs of other women, other men twice their size, pushing them forward and upward. They stayed at the bottoms of the biggest mountains along the route, the mountains they knew we'd never climb on our own, and they carried us. One at a time. Then back down for another, and another, and another. 'Til we were all on the other side of the mountain, together.

I later learned that they were called the AIDS angels. They were so sick. Many were dying of AIDS. But they were at every AIDS ride nationwide. Waiting to help the healthy riders over mountains.

Do you see? They were dying. But they were the strongest ones. The weak will be the strong. I still don't understand it. But when those men carried me to the tops of those mountains, I felt heaven.

When we arrived in D.C., to our finish line, I felt heaven again. There were thousands of us and thousands of them. The streets of D.C. were lined—ten, twelve, twenty people deep, cheering and screaming and crying, and the sound of the joy was deafening. It all became white noise, so through my tears I just watched them, because I couldn't hear them anymore. They showed up for us because we'd shown up for love. Because we'd done something really, really hard, and they wanted to say thank-you, and be a part of it all. I saw my friends there, in the crowd, with signs that said, "WE'RE SO PROUD OF YOU, G!" And I saw Sister and Bubba and Tisha and they were holding signs too, but I don't remember what they said because I can only remember their faces—overwhelmed with the goodness and the power of the moment. The crowds whistled and rang bells and yelled *WE LOVE YOU!* through megaphones. Cheerleading squads leaped and fire trucks blared their sirens and kids held signs that said: *"GOD BLESS YOU, HEROES—GOD BLESS US ALL,"* and there was no rider, not to the left or the right or behind or in front of me, who was not weeping. When we could steady ourselves long enough, we'd grab the hand of the rider beside us because it was too much to take in alone. And our tears and sweat would get all mixed up with the tears and the sweat of the others. And we'd grab the hands of the children who wanted to touch us and pass on the tears and the sweat. And it didn't matter anymore if we were gay or straight or young or old or healthy or dying. We'd been through something real. It had hurt like hell, but we we'd finished. Together.

Namaste

Why Not Be Polite?

Everyone
Is God speaking.
Why not be polite and
Listen to
Him?

—Hafiz

I love God, whoever he is, and I'd really like to get closer to him. I've been thinking about how one of the simplest ways to get close to a woman is to be good to her children. To be kind and gentle and to pay close attention to the things that make them special. To try to see her children the way she sees her children. And how God made us in his image. How he is the mother and father of all of us. So I wonder if that would be the best way to get closer to him too. By being kind and gentle to his children and noticing all of the things that make them special. So many of us spend our time trying to find God in books, but maybe the simplest way to God is directly through the hearts of his children.

Recently a friend sent me a book called *Nomaskar*, which was written by a priest who followed Mother Teresa and studied her spirituality. I love Mother Teresa. I love her for what she did and, more important, *why* she did it. I believe she was living according to the Truth, so I try to pay close attention to her.

The reason that Mother Teresa served the lepers and destitute and dying in the streets of Calcutta was not because Jesus told her to; it was because *Jesus* was leprous and destitute and dying in the streets of Calcutta. And since she worshipped Jesus as God, she figured she should probably go help him, because it didn't make a lot of sense to worship God in church while he was dying alone in the streets. And she believed that it was silly to weep when thinking about Jesus being crucified two thousand years ago, yet not weep while watching Jesus crucified today, on the streets of Calcutta or Haiti or D.C. or in the high school hallway.

Mother Teresa saw God in every human being, and when she held a dying leper and dressed his wounds, she did not *imagine* that she was helping Jesus die with dignity, she really *was* helping Jesus die with dignity. She was holding, as she would have said, "Jesus in the distressing disguise of the poor." She understood that everyone is Jesus. She understood the meaning of the word *Nomaskar,* or *Namaste,* which means "the divine light in me sees and honors the divine light in you." God in me recognizes God in you. And the God in me *honors* the God in you. So when she encountered a person, she would fold her hands, bow her head, and say, "Namaste." And when she wanted to see God, she didn't look *up and away;* she looked into the eyes of the person sitting next to her. Which is harder. Better.

So. I've talked to God about it, and I am *sooooooo* not going to Calcutta. Not really my bag, baby. I'm a Sister of *Sister* . . . not a Sister of Charity. You understand.

But I watch the news and my friends closely, and I hear the sadness in people's stories and the loneliness in their hearts and the pain of their pasts, so I know that *Calcutta is everywhere.* All of us live in some sort of poverty. Poverty of hope, poverty of peace, poverty of love. We are all poor in one way or another. Mama T. used to call material poverty the easiest poverty to alleviate. Everyone is suffering. And since everyone is God, I'd like to be kind, and at the very least not add to people's pain.

So I decided to start bowing to everyone who crossed my path. Just a little teeny bow of my head. Just enough to remind myself not to be a jerk, since no matter who I'm talking to, whether it's a child, or a principal, or a gas station attendant, or a frenemy, or Craig, it's GOD I'm talking to.

And as I bow, I say, *Namaste. God in me recognizes and honors God in you.*

I just *think* Namaste in my head, like the way Orthodox Jews wear a yarmulke to remind themselves that they are living under the hand of God. Or how Muslims pray five times a day to remind themselves of whom they serve. The world and the people in it are so beautiful when you're awake. And so the bowing and the silent Namaste is just a little practice to remind myself what's real. What an amazing life I'm leading and what a gift the people I meet are to me.

I know all of this might sound a little nuts, but I have decided that I am just *over* worrying about that. Robin P. Williams said, "You're only given a spark of madness. You mustn't lose it." And maybe the world needs some crazy love. So I am embracing my spark of madness. Fanning it, even. And I'm *bowing*. And something's happening because of it. It's *working*. I'm starting to see God everywhere.

It's like that little bow of my head snaps me out of the horrible trance I allow myself to get lulled into each day, in which I forget that *everything and everyone is magic. Including me. Namaste.*

Hard

This way of life—living *out loud*—is hard. It's good, in many, many ways, but it's hard too. Most of the people who read my stories don't know me, but many do. And it's tough, sometimes, on the people who know me. It's hard on my family and my friends. Sometimes I wonder if it's hard on my poor neighbors, who have to know SO MUCH about us. When I see them outside and they say, "How are you?" it's funny, because they already know. It makes us closer and further apart somehow. At this point, when I meet someone new, I know immediately, by her face, whether she reads my work. When someone invites me to coffee, I want to say, "Perfect. Could you bring along four hundred extremely personal essays about your life so we can start on even ground?"

In many ways living out loud is the hardest on *me*.

I mostly love writing. It serves me, heals me, and satisfies the creative cat constantly clawing at my insides, trying to get out. It helps me make sense of things and holds me accountable to myself.

Recently I wrote an essay about my hopes and dreams, and I included in it my belief that my fourth child is in Rwanda. This is the response I received from one of my readers: *"Hi Glennon . . . may I make a gentle reminder that you DO have four children? Please don't discount the one you chose not to raise on this earth. I'm wondering if that's part of your desire to adopt, to make up for that decision?"*

My, my, my.

First—let us be clear, this person had every right to have this response. Most of my readers have agreed to an unwritten rule that we don't use the truths I tell against me. But no one's forced to follow this rule. I walk onto this field every day without armor or weapons, by choice, and so the risk is that every once in a while, someone will shoot. It happens. It hurts, and it always, always makes me want to quit writing. But I don't. When I want to shut off my computer, take my life back as my own, curl up into a protective roly-poly ball, I don't. I come back to the page because I want to keep loving and remaining open, even though neither love nor openness is easy.

Love is not warm and fuzzy or sweet and sticky. Real love is **tough as nails**. It's having your heart ripped out, putting it back together, and the next day, offering it back to the same world that just tore it up. It's running toward pain and grief and brokenness instead of away from it. It's turning the other cheek 'til you get whiplash. It's resisting the overwhelming desire to quit, to save yourself *for* yourself. It's exhausting and uncomfortable. Sometimes it's ugly, like using your bare hands to search for gold in piles of crap.

I try to live my life the same way that a carpenter who lived two thousand years ago lived his. Once he stood on a hilltop and explained how to *love well* to a huge group of people hanging onto his every word, shocked by the countercultural ideas he was suggesting. And they recognized what he was saying as the Truth. He wasn't telling them anything new, actually. He was just reminding them of everything that was already written onto their hearts.

The first time I read the things Jesus said about love, it all rang so true to me that my heart about exploded. It rang hard but true. Jesus said that when someone hurts you, you should love that person, and you should turn the other cheek over and over and over again. Seven times seventy times, I think. I've been writing for over five years, so I've got to be getting close to that number. Let's just say that the four hundredth and ninety-first reader who tries to hurt my feelings is going to get his ASS KICKED.

But the person who questioned my desire to adopt is not lucky five hundred and thirty-nine. So, since my Jesus insists, I must turn the other cheek. The beautiful thing about turning the other cheek is that it forces you to break eye contact with the person who has slapped you, and this little turn changes your perspective. Now, all of sudden, you are looking away, forward, to something better, more beautiful, and your heartbeat settles, and your palms stop sweating.

So here I am. I've turned. I have a new perspective. I have tried to do what my friend Meghan often suggests, which is to "listen for the love" in what's said to me. And so I'll try to address this reader with love.

I have no doubt that my abortion has something to do with my desire to adopt. As do my parents' teachings that we belong to each other, and Sister's passion for the powerless, and my gift at mothering, and the extra money and other resources that God's given me to share, and my faith, and my relationship with my husband, and my teaching experiences with underprivileged children, and on and on and on. My dreams are the sum total of everything that has ever happened to me, everyone I've ever met, every book I've ever read, every friend I've loved, every mistake I've made, and every song I've sung. So I would be silly to pretend to be certain that the two, abortion and adoption, are entirely unrelated. Everything is related to everything, obviously.

What begs to be addressed here is the reader's suggestion that through adoption, I'd be assuaging my guilt for my abortion.

Please, let me be clear: *I don't have any shame about my abortion.* None. I know that's hard for some people to hear, because in some circles, if you are a Christian and abortion has been a part of your life, you are supposed to beat your chest and gnash your teeth and repent and then join crusades to end abortion by any means necessary, and speak through tears to large and small groups of people and swear to them that abortion was the worst mistake you've ever made and explain that you pray for your dead baby in heaven every night. THEN your sinner-self will be embraced and used as a poster girl. Literally, likely.

But I won't say or do any of that, ever. Because none of that is true, *for me.* I know it's true for some, and I respect that each has her own path. But it's not true for me. I did the best I could at the time with the resources I felt I had. I've apologized, yes—but mostly to myself. I feel sad for the lost girl I was, and I am fiercely protective of that precious me who had to go through that scary day and the days that preceded and followed. Far from ashamed, I'm really quite proud of her for making it through. I don't feel ashamed. I feel forgiven and whole, and I know that God never let go of my hand before, during, or after my abortion. God and I are clear on this issue.

As Maya Angelou says. "I did then what I knew how to do. Now that I know better, I do better." Amen. There is no room for shame or regret in my life. I'm too full. I am too forgiven, too adored, too fully loved, too full of ideas and dreams and passion to waste my precious life pretending to be crippled by something that is imaginary, like shame. Shame is an illusion. It disappears so easily.

Hard

I have confused feelings about the *abortion issue*. I think that "issues" like abortion are really just "people," so it's best to think of them as such. One at a time. One person at a time. I don't feel shame about my abortion. But I don't love abortion either. And/ Both. I think there are probably better ways.

But I also think that if you really, really hate abortion, it might be nice to volunteer at a Boys and Girls Club and become a mentor, to offer a kid another way to experience love and connection so she doesn't go looking for it in the wrong places. It might be wise to try to jump into the mix before it's too late. I think the picket lines at the clinics might be a little too late. Offering unsolicited suggestions to a writer who had an abortion more than a decade ago is *certainly* too late.

As for me, in keeping with the one-person-at-a-time theory, I think that if a young friend confided in me that she was pregnant and was considering an abortion, Craig and I would hold her and tell her that she was loved and that she had many choices.

We would tell her that she could live with us, and we would make sure she was taken care of, physically and financially, and that if she wanted to keep the baby, we would help her start her life.

We would also tell her that if she didn't want to raise the baby, we'd raise the baby for her.

And if she decided that abortion was the only way, we would hold her hand and love her through it and demand that she know that she was as loved and adored the moment after the abortion as she was on the day she was born.

The only meaningful thing we can offer one another is love. Not advice, not questions about our choices, not suggestions for the future, just love.

What D'Ya Know?

I ran into an old friend yesterday who told me that she reads my stories and loves them. She said, *thank you so much for writing.* Instead of squirming and making up a million reasons to reject her gratitude, I replied, *"You are so welcome."* Learning how to gracefully accept criticism and compliments is hard, but I'm trying.

Then she said: *Do you ever worry that you might share too much? Do you worry that when you need to go back to work, no one will hire you because of your festive past?*

Wow. Nope. Never worried about that.

I rushed home and yelled up the stairs: *HUSBAND! Do you ever worry that when I need to go back to work, no one will hire me because I've told the world all about my festive past?*

Husband: I mean, I've considered it.

Me: *Why didn't you ever mention anything to me?*

Husband: It was too late.

Me: *Oh.*

Hm.

It seems that I may have rendered myself *eternally unemployable* by telling the truth.

I just have one thing to say about this: ARE THE UNEXPECTED BLESSINGS OF WRITING JUST NEVERENDING???????

I could die of excitement. I might have to start writing about a few things I *haven't even done* just to seal the deal.

Retired! Retired! Forever retired!!! Yoga pants forever!!! Joy.

On Profanity

> Under certain circumstances, profanity provides a relief
> denied even to prayer.
>
> —Mark Twain

I receive plenty of mail from concerned readers about my occa-
sional use of profanity. They believe God is offended by it, so
they are too. I love my readers, and when they are hurt by my
writing, I think hard about that.

Maybe God is up in heaven keeping lists of bad words and
tallying how many times we say each one. Maybe those arbitrary
four-letter words that are different in every country, culture, and
era are the unwholesome, crude talk that the Bible insists we
avoid. Maybe.

Or maybe God's actually referring to the most harmful kind
of talk in which people of light can participate: gossip talk and
ungrateful talk and racist and sexist and classist talk and sarcasm
and snide, dismissive, apathetic remarks and maybe even nasty
phrases like *more* and *not my problem* and *us/them* and *looking out
for number one* and the scariest phrase of all, *the deserving poor.* As
if there is any other kind of poor?

Or maybe he's talking about language intended to exclude people. Religious talk does that sometimes. Religious words can be

used to make some people feel in and other people feel out. If they're used that way, to suggest that some people are "God people" and others aren't, then I think religious words become profane.

And you know, if four-letter words are used in a way that helps a sister express herself, tell her truth, make her art, relate to other people, get it OUT, then I think Jesus would dig it. I really do. I think Jesus likes REAL, whatever form in which it comes. We've each got deep wells of profanity inside us—deep enough to keep us busy bailing our own wells before dipping into anybody else's.

I heard a radio sermon recently given by the minister of one of the largest churches in the country. He was passionately insisting that Christians should protect themselves from *secular* music. He used the example of rap and discussed its profanity with disgust. He said that adult Christians should stay away from it at all costs, or it could *corrupt them.*

It really got to me, that sermon.

Sometimes I listen to gangster rap. Don't laugh. I like art, any art that is true and raw and real, and sometimes rap fits the bill. Sometimes as I listen to a song, an angry song, about poverty and dead ends and the hopelessness and the violence that are the inevitable results, I think, *Jesus would love this song.* I don't think he'd cover his ears and turn up his nose and run away because of the crudeness. I don't think the coarseness would *offend* him. As a matter of fact, the people who were a little rough around the edges never offended Jesus. The shiny perfect Pharisees did, though. He called them vipers and white-washed tombs. Poisonous. Perfect and shiny outside, decaying on the inside.

If Jesus were that pastor, I don't think he'd tell his people to turn off the radio. I think he'd tell them to *turn it up and listen,* even if it made them uncomfortable. He'd tell them to *listen* to the stories of people who've been oppressed and marginalized and are crying out for someone to hear them and step in. He'd say, *"Sounds a lot like the Psalms, doesn't it?"* And instead of allowing his followers to comfort themselves by creating false groups of us/them (they are so bad/we are so good; we must not become contaminated!), I think Jesus might ask them to listen to the despair and anger and to ask themselves, *How am I part of this problem? What can I, as a neighbor, do to help level the playing field?* Jesus didn't say: "Love your neighbor, unless he offends you." I'm not sure that being offended is a luxury that people who've been commanded to love each other can enjoy. Otherwise we are in danger of becoming people who were born on third base, peeved that those not issued a ticket into the ballpark refuse to complain sweetly enough.

I just think that if this pastor was so very upset by poverty and the agony it causes, maybe instead of suggesting that his well-off congregation flee from it, he might have suggested that they skip the mall and lunch after church and use the time and money to serve some meals to the poor instead. Maybe they could have gone to meet some of these gangsters. Maybe they could have headed to the prisons or streets, like Jesus did, instead of walking away.

There was a town in Jesus's day called Samaria. Jews did NOT go to Samaria. Samarians were the "others" back then. Morally questionable, you know. Samaria was the *wrong side of the tracks*. Jews would add lots of time to their trips just to walk *around* Samaria. But the gospels are careful to mention that whenever Jesus traveled, he walked right *through* Samaria.

Always *right through it,* that Jesus. Rolling deep with his entourage, the twelve disciples. *Laaaaiiiid back. With their minds on their manna and their manna on their minds.*

Jesus actually met one of his favorite people in Samaria, someone he used as an example of how to love your neighbor—the Good Samaritan. Maybe gangster rap is like Samaria. Maybe "profane" blogs are. Maybe a lot of places we avoid are. Maybe there are people we can learn from in these places.

A minister recently sent me this quote: "The problem with the faith pool these days is that all the noise is coming from the shallow end. I waded into the deep end, and that has made all the difference."

It's easy to spend time in the shallow end of faith. It's not a real commitment. You can just hop in, stand around in tight circles, and people-watch. You can examine your nails, read, reread, and catch up on all the gossip. You can talk and talk and talk and come to a great many conclusions and decisions and still maintain your hairstyle and even avoid smudging your makeup. This is important because you never know when someone will pull out a camera. You can spend an entire comfortable life there, really, just standing around being heard. You never even have to learn to *swim* in the shallow end. Good times.

I think the reason we don't hear from the people in the deep end as often is because *they're actually swimming.* In the deep end, you have to keep moving. It's hard to look cool. It's tiring and scary even, since it's just you and your head and your heart in the silence of the depths. There's not much chatting or safety in numbers in the deep end. You have to spend most of your time there alone. And it's impossible to get any solid footing. You just have to trust that the water will hold you, and you have no other choice but to flail about and gasp for air and get soaking wet, head to toe.

There are these monks called the Benedictines, and they live in monasteries all over the world and follow the Rule, which is a set of ideas about living in community written by St. Benedict a long, long time ago. I study this Rule before handling conflicts in my heart, friendships, home, and art. Here's one of my favorite parts of Benedict's Rule:

"Persevere. Bear with great patience each other's infirmities of body or behavior. And when the thorns of contention arise, daily forgive, and be ready to accept forgiveness."

If you are someone who considers cursing to be a weakness, please bear with us cursers with great patience, and daily forgive us. If you are someone who considers intolerance for cursing a weakness, please bear with us with great patience and daily forgive us. Persevere. Try to see through to the God in us. Swim in the deep end. As St. Benedictine says, "Listen with the ear of the heart."

Gifts Are Bridges

Don't ask what the world needs. Ask what makes you
come alive, and go do it. Because what the world needs
is people who have come alive.

—Howard Thurman

I think God gives us each a gift or two so that we have something
special to offer to others. But sometimes we make the mistake of
assuming that the things we're good at are common to everyone.
We don't recognize that our gifts are unique and therefore worth
offering. For example, I am a good writer and a good listener.
When my friends think of me, they think, "Glennon—she's a
good writer and a good listener." But I never knew these skills
were unusual until one afternoon in my friend Michelle's kitchen.

We were talking about an upcoming party and I said: "You
know, Michelle, parties stress me out because everyone brings
delicious fancy dishes to share and I don't really even **own** any
dishes to put a dish **on** even if I **wanted** to make a dish. Which
I don't, by the way. So sometimes I avoid gatherings just because
I'm too annoyed about all the dish bringing. I mean, even stopping at the store for a bag of chips seems overwhelming to me. I
don't know why. I have a sign in my house that says, 'WE CAN
DO HARD THINGS,' and sometimes I think I should add a

second one below it that says, 'BUT WE CANNOT DO EASY THINGS.'"

And Michelle said, "Yeah. You don't bring amazing dishes. But you know what you do bring? You have a way of making me feel important when we talk. You really listen to me. That's why I like having you at our parties. You are a great listener."

And I thought, hmmmm.

Now, when people invite me to things and they ask what I'll bring, I say: "I will bring my amazing listening ears." If they love me, this will be fine with them. They'll understand. If it is not fine with them, they will stop inviting me to things. Win-win.

Another one of my gifts is writing.

Dana is one of my dearest, best friends on earth. Dana lost her daddy recently. It was shocking and horrifying, and it still is. Dana is a daddy's girl, and she honored her father and their relationship by writing and delivering the eulogy at his memorial service. Can you imagine? A week after she lost him, she stood up in front of hundreds of his friends and her family and spoke eloquently of his greatness and their loss. It was one of the most remarkable things I've ever seen. Certainly one of the bravest. Heroic, really.

A few nights before the memorial, Dana asked me to revise her eulogy for her father. It's a good thing she did, because after reading it several times with a very critical eye, I had to admit that in my expert writing opinion, she should consider changing the *but* in the third paragraph to an *and*. Dana didn't really need me at all. But she thought of me because she knows I'm a writer. And since I'm a writer, I got invited into one of the most important moments in her family's life. It was such an honor to read that love letter to her daddy. To read it first. To feel, at the memorial, that I was up there on the altar with her.

That got me thinking about all the other ways that writing has served as an invitation into important moments of my friend's lives.

My friend Joey and her fiancé Brock invited me to help write their wedding vows. Those were pretty damn good vows. Now I kind of feel like all three of us are married to each other—Joey, Brock, and me. The gift of writing, it turns out, has been my ticket into others' lives.

And I've realized that these bridges go two ways: others' gifts are their tickets into my life as well.

My friend Gena has a gift for hostessing. Gena doesn't just use her beautiful home to hostess; she uses her whole heart. She throws opens her doors and invites people to step inside and celebrate life. Her gift is celebration, creating an atmosphere in her home and presence in which her friends feel loved and honored. She has hosted each of my last four birthday parties, and she hosts a huge Christmas party every year for all of us. Being a hostess doesn't stress her out; she loves it. It's her gift—welcoming people. And because she offers it to me, Gena's face will be front and center in our family's celebration memories forever. Because of her gift, there are many, many bridges between Gena and me.

And then there's Sister's best friend, Allison. Allison is an artist, and her medium is the camera. She feels at home behind the camera, and God has given her the gift of noticing important moments and capturing them. So her friends and family invite her into their important days to help them grab the magical parts and keep them forever. And Allison becomes a part of those days, those memories, forever. She's all tangled up in there. It's funny: Allison is quiet at events—she's more of an "ahh, there you are" person than a "HEY! Here I am!" person, but when you look at her photographs, you realize that she was actually more there than anyone else. She detected and documented every meaningful moment.

I think sometimes we get confused and believe that our gift must bring us money or success or fame. Sometimes those things do happen, but not usually. The only thing a gift needs to do is bring you joy. You must find the thing that brings you joy in the doing of that thing, and not worry about the outcome. Your gift might be crucial and obviously helpful, like being a good listener, or it might be odd and unique. For example, one of Sister's many gifts is finding incredible deals at thrift stores. She dresses like a movie star, and every time someone compliments her on a fabulous blouse, her face lights up and she yells, "Fifty cents! I got it for fifty cents!" Then she usually tries to give the shirt to the person who offered the compliment, which gets a little awkward. Her gift helps the world because she always shops at Goodwill, so her shopping is like charity work, and buying recycled clothes is very green. But really, the important thing is that it makes her feel alive. It's a gift. It brings her joy and satisfaction. Happier people make a better world.

Writing brings me joy and satisfaction. My gift has happened to turn into a career, and parts of that are wonderful and parts of that are not. I am happiest not when I am congratulated on a book deal, but when I have finished an essay that says what I mean. That's all. Expressing myself effectively brings me great joy. You will know your gift because it will bring you joy and satisfaction, even if it's hard for you to do. You will go about using your gift quietly, and eventually someone might notice and ask you to share your gift. If you agree to share, your gift will become a bridge. I suppose it's possible that no one will ever ask, or that you will be too afraid to accept. Consider Emily Dickinson. Her gift was poetry, but she kept that gift to herself. Then she died, and her writing was found, and her gift became a bridge into millions of hearts. I think it's pretty hard to keep a gift from becoming a bridge, somehow, someday, someway—if we use it. Because I think that God must really want us to connect with each other. He must want us to become a part of each other's lives and memories, and he must want our hearts to get all tangled up with other hearts. We are each an island, but he gives us gifts to use as bridges into each other's lives. When we lay down our gift, we walk right over it and straight into another heart.

Hostressing

"True hospitality is welcoming the stranger on her own terms. This kind of hospitality can only be offered by those who've found the center of their lives in their own hearts."

—Henri Nouwen

The thing about the bridges is that I feel more comfortable walking over them and entering other people's lives than inviting them into mine. For example, I am terrified of allowing people into my house. Sometimes when I hear a knock on the door, I *hide* in my bathroom until the knocking stops.

Inviting *others* into my home—it's such an intimate act. I mean, our home is *where we live*. It's where we keep all of our Meltony messes and stains and smells and dust. And I've heard that 99 percent of dust is dead skin cells. Dead Melton skin cells? *Please, come in and sit among our family's dead skin cells.* Seems odd. Showing outsiders our insides is a scary *big deal* to me. I'm better at opening up figuratively, through my writing. The *real* thing in the real world makes me twitch and sweat.

Last week my cousins stopped by unannounced, and while they went upstairs to see the kids' rooms, I started my deep, cleansing breaths while frantically scrounging through the empty pantry. I grabbed a box of pasta and a bottle of vinegar. Then I dropped them and grabbed Craig by the shoulders instead. I looked deep into his eyes and said: *"Oh my **God!** What do people eat??"*

Because that's the thing. I just don't know. I don't know what people eat.

And even if I *did* know what people eat, I wouldn't know how to *make* those things. And even if I *could* make those things, I wouldn't have the *stuff* needed to serve those things. Each time a guest rifles through my pantry (yikes! sweat!), she casually asks, "Hey G, where is your . . ." Fill in the blank. Trivet? Cheese cutter? Curry? And I have to say, "Whatever *that thing you just said* is, I don't have it."

Sister came over to cook dinner recently, which she does occasionally for the sake of the children, and she yelled from the kitchen, "Glennon, where are your PANS?" and I yelled back, "I don't have one." And after that shocked silence to which I've become *well accustomed,* she yelled back, "You don't own **A** pan? *How do you cook without a single pan?*" And I said, *"Yeah. I know, IT'S REALLY HARD."* And then she walked into the family room and stared at me in disbelief for a good two minutes. When she finally spoke, she said something about how she has MULTIPLE PANS FOR VARIOUS PURPOSES and how I COULD SIMPLY NOT *NOT* have a single pan in my home.

I took a deep breath and said, "Give me a *break.* So I don't have a pan? So what? It's not like there's anything I can *do about it.* Every day I pray the serenity prayer, 'Allow me to accept the things I cannot change,' and then I *accept the fact that I do not have a pan.* Also, if we're being honest here, I think you're being a bit judgmental. Just because you're a 'multiple pan owner' doesn't mean that we all must join you in your life of excess. Sister, there are children starving in Africa, actually *at my house too*, and you're walking around with your head in the clouds, judging the panless and gloating about your *multiple pans.*"

Sister took a deep breath, walked back to the kitchen, and called for pizza delivery.

So you see, any sort of hostessing that involves a pan is out of the question. Water is another challenge. I have noticed that when people come over, they tend to want water. All of my glasses still look dirty when I get them out of the dishwasher, and I'm afraid if I serve my guests water from a dirty glass, they'll think that my family and I are dirty too. So I buy bottled water. But then I'm afraid that if I serve guests bottled water, they'll think I'm environmentally irresponsible. It's a risk either way, really. So I analyze each guest and try to predict which type of water will offend her less. Tree huggers get dirty glasses and fancy-pantses get bottles.

And wine. *Dear Lord. Please* don't ask for wine. During my drinking days, I drank wine from the box, but it's been suggested to me that serving boxed wine to guests when one is in one's mid- to late thirties is tacky. But I never learned how to uncork a bottle. Who could afford *corked bottles* back in the day? Additionally, all my wine glasses have these Saturny *rings* around them. Often, these rings are accompanied by leftover lip gloss stains. Thanks for doing your job, *dishwasher. What is it that you actually do around here, anyway?* And the *crumbs* in the silverware drawer, the toilets my angels forgot to flush, the dog poop in the backyard that Craig missed. I just get sweaty about all of it. And so I allow my fear of embarrassment to stop me from hostessing anyone.

I tell myself it's fine, it's just not "my thing," but I actually think that's a weak excuse. Because there are things we should do, regardless of whether they are our favorite "things" or not, because they help us grow and rest and connect with other people. Like fresh air—people should get some each day whether they want to or not. It helps. And telling the truth. That's hard, but people should do it anyway. Fresh air isn't just for outdoorsy people, telling the truth isn't just for honest people, and hospitality isn't just for Martha Stewarty people. I think inviting people into your home, whether it's an impeccable mansion or a rusty old shack, is probably an important practice. I think we're supposed to take deep breaths, tell the truth, and keep our hearts, minds, and spaces *open* to others, whether these things are easy for us or not. Because hospitality is not about fancy table settings, just like writing isn't about fancy words. They are both about letting people *see you*. Letting people in *now*, not waiting until things are perfect. So deep down, I think that humoring my hostess phobia is selfish, prideful, and lazy of me. And I'm afraid that I'm missing out on something awesome, since every spiritual practice eventually delivers a big blessing.

In the Bible, there is a story about the time Jesus and his twelve disciples came to visit the home of two sisters, Mary and Martha. Martha gets very busy and harried with all the preparations because, I mean, *Jesus plus twelve?? JESUS. Talk about hostess.* Martha starts cooking and cleaning and trying to find all of her hostessy things and working herself into a frenzy. Then she notices that her younger sister, Mary, is just sitting there at Jesus's feet. Mary's not cooking, not cleaning, not hustling or bustling or serving anything to anybody. She's just resting and listening and soaking in Jesus's company. And Martha is still in the kitchen grabbing her hubby's shoulders and yelling, *"WHAT DO GODS AND DISCIPLES EAT?"* And the thing is that she is so busy trying to make things perfect for Jesus that she is missing him. She is missing his visit entirely, and she is miserable. When she's finally had enough, Martha says to Jesus, *"JESUS CHRIST! Can you please tell my sister to HELP ME?? I'm all on my own here. And there are **thirteen** of you!"* And Jesus says something awesome. He says, *"Martha, you are worried about so many things. Mary has chosen the better part, and it won't be taken from her."*

The better part of what? The better part of hospitality? Is it possible that true hospitality is not about perfect food or fancy furniture? Could the better part of hospitality be *listening*? If you can't do both, could the *better part* be focusing on your guest instead of trying to impress or even *feed* him? Could the *better place* be the family room, at the foot of your guest, instead of tucked away in the kitchen? *Maybe.* Maybe hostessing is not really about the host, but the guest. Maybe it's a sacred spiritual practice because every single person who crosses our doorsteps is a gift, is *Jesus* really. And each guest has something to teach us if we're present enough to learn. Maybe hospitality is not about my home, or my food, or my *lack of stuff.* Maybe it's just about soaking people in.

After letting *this* new idea soak in for a few days, I told Craig that I was going to take the plunge. I was going to throw a party for my best friends. Craig thought it was a great idea because we'd have lots of excuses to be unprepared since we'd just moved into our new house. Yes, I said, *brilliant!* We will do this *our way. Not Martha Stewart's way or biblical Martha's way. Our way.*

So I wrote up an e-mail invitation and sent it to all of my best friends:

Dearest Friends,

I have decided to face my hostressing issue by having you all over the week after we move in to our new home. Please note the following things.

217

Bring Food. I don't have any. Bring a seat. We don't have many. No fabrics other than flannel will be permitted to cross my door step. Pajamas, please—don't be a show-off. Use the bathroom before you come, because I am all out of Windex. Whatever the thing is you like to drink, please bring that thing. Also bring something to drink that thing out of. I can't deal with the glasses situation right now. Too many different types of glasses. It's ridiculous, if you want my opinion. Also. At nine o'clock you will say, "We should go" and I will say, "No, please stay!" **Don't stay. GO.** I'm really, really tired and I'm just trying to be polite because etiquette is extremely important to me.

LYLAS,
G

All of my best friends came to my unparty. They *all* came in their jammies, bearing snacks and drinks and smiles.

We ate their food and drank their drinks and somebody *else* opened the wine, thank God. And they all squeezed onto my one and only couch and I sat at their feet because I'm a floor sitter. All evening, I soaked them in. Looking up at all my friends laughing and comfortable, I realized, *I can handle this.* I don't have to miss out on this anymore because *they're all the way in* and they love me anyway, maybe even more than they did before. The whole evening felt so warm and wonderful, I didn't even get mad when they stayed until 9:15.

And now, I am a hostess. Without the r.

Room for One More

Craig and I are considering becoming official members of our neighborhood church. This is a big deal for us, because a few years ago we promised ourselves we wouldn't choose a denomination. We couldn't imagine the need for it. Still can't, really. We consider ourselves religious rolling stones. We find it important to be the leaders of our family's faith life instead of passing off that job. We worry that blindly following others' interpretations of God and scripture can get dangerous. God can speak to each of us directly, after all.

But we've fallen for this little church, and we started wondering if our religious "freedom" wasn't just another word for nothing left to lose. Because we know that any faith worth a damn is a faith worked out over a lifetime of relationships with other people. *Church* is just a commitment to try to live a life of a certain quality—a life of love, of humility, of service—alongside others for whom you will care and allow to care for you, even when that's difficult. It's a group of regular old humans trying to love each other and the world in superhuman ways. And so it's a hard way of life, but to me, it's the only way of life that makes any sense. When people ask me if faith, if church, is comforting to me, I say, "Sort of." But mostly it's challenging.

Still, I was afraid to join this new church. Because I don't want to pretend to believe anything I don't believe. I don't want to pretend to not have doubts. And I don't want my children to be taught things about God that I'll have to undo. Before I joined any church, I needed permission from whomever was in charge to be different.

So I invited one of the ministers over to my house.

I was scared.

We talked for two hours. I told her all of my concerns. I wanted to join her church, but first, I wanted to make sure she wanted me. I warned her that I am a troublemaker.

I told her that I love Jesus madly and deeply, but my problem always seemed to be that I understand him *quite* differently than many other Christians do. And I love these other Christians, so I didn't want offend them. I suggested that maybe it was better for me to remain unattached to any particular church rather than disrupt a perfectly lovely one.

I explained that I had all kinds of doubts and questions and negative feelings about the church's role throughout history. But I told her I still loved the church. I felt kind of like St. Augustine, who said, "The church is a whore, but she's my mother." If I were to become a member of her church, I would need permission to speak my mind respectfully but freely. I would need permission to be myself. I wanted her to know all the things I believe because I knew that eventually they were all going to come out of *my* mouth in *her* church.

My minister said she understood, and she wanted me. She likes me, I think. She said our church would fit me just fine. She doesn't mind a troublemaker or two in her fold. She said she had room for one more.

So we'll see. My biggest fear when entering any church is always, *"Oh, Jesus. What are they going to teach my babies about*

God?" So guess what I did? I signed up to teach Sunday school. And I've already fallen in love with my Sunday school team. I'm not sure they know I'm a troublemaker yet, though. God help them.

LETTING GO

Treasure Hunt

Although I'm fascinated by the idea and have been reading about the subject for years, I still don't understand what Zen is. For now, let's oversimplify and agree that Zen is perfect peace derived from the transcendence of human suffering through meditation. Imagine the smiling Buddha, the one who holds the secret to life: he is enlightened, beyond desire, beyond frustration, beyond suffering. Zen. If there is one word that represents the opposite of how I experience life, it's *Zen*.

In fact, I find life to be constantly and excruciatingly difficult. A while ago Sister told me about a mother who came to her East African law office and explained that her five-year-old daughter had been raped by a neighbor. This mother had tried for two weeks to have the rapist arrested and get her daughter free medical attention, since she didn't have the two dollars to cover her care. Because she kept getting turned away, she couldn't work for two weeks, and her five children were home starving—still living next door to the rapist.

In *Night*, by Elie Wiesel, a Holocaust survivor describes watching Nazis throw living Jewish babies into fiery ditches and grown, educated, uniformed men publicly hang Jewish children.

I have three dear friends who've watched their marriages, parents' health, and dreams for their families crumble in front of them this month.

And the oil spills, the animals, our earth—*Jesus*. How will our children forgive us for continuing on like we have planets to spare?

As the curtains are lifted and we discover the greed, carelessness, and apathy that led to all of these disasters, I just want to walk outside and scream forever. But how can I rail against it all when I sense so much of that same greed, carelessness and apathy inside of me?

The paralyzing pain and impossibility of life is why I believe that there is something True about Jesus. Not Christianity, necessarily, the way it has come to be understood, but Jesus. His story. The cross. Because when I look at that man hanging lifeless and bloody, nailed to the cross, I understand him to be *just* the symbol that a God who knows the states of our hearts and our world would send to represent the Truth. To make us feel understood. Loved, even.

As I finished reading *Night,* forever changed, I imagined Elie Wiesel, after the war, sitting in my living room and telling me the story of how the Nazis killed his family.

He would tell me that this happened to thousands of families. While the Earth kept spinning. While people all over the planet kept eating their breakfasts and getting dressed and going to work and having picnics and listening to the radio. And how it's still happening now. Right now, to powerless people all over the world. How humanity has not learned from his family, from his people's suffering. That our world has yet to say . . . **ENOUGH.**

But he would add that he still has hope. That despair is not an option. And then the room would get quiet.

I can't imagine, for the life of me, showing the young Wiesel the smiling Buddha. I cannot imagine suggesting to him that his suffering could possibly be *transcended*. I can only imagine showing him a picture of Jesus hanging on the cross, bloody and beaten and mocked and spit upon and abandoned and God forsaken. And I can only imagine whispering, with trembling hands and voice: *Is this how you feel?*

I'm curious about people who have found a way to transcend the world's collective pain and their own personal suffering. But I *respect* people who don't try to escape permanently. Who run *toward* the pain. Who allow themselves to suffer with others, to become brokenhearted. I respect people who, enlightened or not, roll up their sleeves and give up their comfortable lives for suffering people. Or who don't do any of those things but pay close enough attention to know and admit and care that life can be brutal. Who understand that their comfortable reality is not enjoyed by all.

Years ago, my hopeful, faithful, joyful minister surprised our congregation by saying: *Life is pain, and anyone who tells you different is trying to sell you something.* I squirmed in my seat and thought . . . Jeez. *How negative.* But now I'm older, and I think . . . *How true.* Life is hard and terrifying and unfair and overwhelming. Life is the cross. And if you think that's overly dramatic, please pay close attention to the evening news. After that, read up on the international child sex trade and spend the next afternoon in your local middle school cafeteria observing how kids who look different are treated. Finally, on your way home, stop by the children's oncology unit at the hospital. Then we'll talk. Life is pain.

BUT.

There is beauty to be found in the pain. Life is brutal, but it's also beautiful. Life is *Brutiful*. So I look hard for the beauty. I try to drown out my fear voice, which wants me to run away from the pain, and listen instead to my love voice, whom I call God, and who is asking me to run *towards* it. To allow my heart to be broken open, because a broken heart is both a badge of honor and the most powerful tool on earth.

That love voice—she'll help you find treasure. But she'll guide you right into the minefields first.

So that's why I write—to find the treasures in the suffering. And as I write, my memories change ever so slightly. Reality and writing work together to create my memories, and the final result is that I remember events more beautifully than they actually happened. Or maybe in writing them down, I'm able to see for the first time how beautiful they really were.

I do not know Zen. I just know gratitude. I am grateful for the beauty in the midst of suffering. I am grateful for the treasure hunt through the minefield of life. Dangerous or not, I don't want out of the minefield. Because truth, and beauty, and God are there.

Jubilee

Let's talk real estate.

Several years ago, Craig and I bought our first single-family home. The home was within a comfortable price range, but we chose an interest-only, adjustable-rate mortgage because back then, we still believed in shortcuts. Recently we woke up and started asking tough questions about our loan—questions like *who* are we really paying each month, and *how much, exactly?* We learned that we were $100,000 underwater, and the details of our loan meant that we could pay our mortgage faithfully 'til the end of time without putting a dent in the principal. We also learned that when our rate adjusted in the very near future, our mortgage would increase by $1,000 per month.

Craig and I worried and agonized and prayed, and we finally decided to sell our house. We planned a short sale, citing a Lyme-induced move as our "hardship." But after breakfast, Craig went to the bank and stood in line behind a single mom who was crying and pleading with the manager to help save her home, which she was about to lose to foreclosure. Her two young children were hanging on her legs, looking more weary and afraid than kids need to look. Craig came home, walked into the kitchen, and said, *"Honey. No short sale. We'll save those for people with real hardships. We'll just cash out everything and start over after the house sells."*

I said, *"What? Let's think this over."*

Craig raised his hot little eyebrow at me, and said, *"G, it's the right thing to do. If we needed to do a short sale, we would. But we don't need to. We have the money. So we'll use it."*

I said, *"But neeeeeed is such a tricky word."*

And Craig said, *"No it's not."*

And I sighed loudly and said, *"Okay,"* and felt terrified and wildly proud to be Craig's girl.

We went to see a financial planner and explained our predicament. He asked questions about our money and marriage and goals, and we told him that our dream of home ownership had been replaced with dreams of peace and freedom. We said that there were things we wanted to do, places we wanted to go, money we wanted to spend and give, moves we wanted to consider, but we felt paralyzed because we'd allowed our mortgage company to become the primary decision maker in our family. We told him that we wanted to know what kind of decisions we'd make if we fired our mortgage company as the boss of us. I told him I wanted Craig to be free of the pressure of our sky-high bills. We shared that we wanted to be more conscious and careful about choosing the companies to which we gave our money. And we said we wanted to live a little simpler, travel a little lighter. He asked us why we didn't just do a short sale, and we explained that we thought short sales were perfect for some, but not for us at this point, since we couldn't honestly say that we didn't have the money. We said we thought the right thing to do was suck it up and start over.

Then we stopped talking and waited for him to tell us we were nuts. But he didn't. He looked at us and said, "I hear you. All of this makes sense to me. You need to be free. I get it. I think you should go for it. And I agree that you should do it without the short sale. You have plenty of time to rebuild, and I believe you will. Free your family, and do it your way."

We put our sweet little house on the market, and it went under contract in two weeks. We brought $140,000 to the table, just to walk away. We left our retirement accounts, our entire savings, and Chase's college fund on the closing company's big fancy brown table.

So we started over, with nothing again.

For now, *starting over* looks like spending a third of our old mortgage on rent. It looks like narrowing our belongings down to what would fit in two small storage units. It looks like shrugging when something breaks, calling our landlord, and waiting for it to get fixed. It sounds like Craig saying *whatever, at least our bills are next to nothing* after losing a big deal at work. It also looks like buying my new hair color at the dollar store. Based on those results, I might suggest finding other corners to cut. But you know, it's actually sort of cute, in a vampirish kind of way. *Whatever.*

Whatever is our new spiritual motto and mantra. *Whatever* is **divine**.

Most important, starting over feels like knowing in the back of our hearts that if we are needed anywhere, anytime, we can go. We're free. And what better use of money is there than to buy freedom?

We live in so much fear about money: *what if* it all goes away, *what if* we're left with nothing, *what if, what if, what if*? We're scared to take risks, to relax even, because *what if* . . . But here's the thing: Craig and I are in the middle of the *what if* right now.

It's all gone. And it's fine. It's better than fine. We might have nothing, but we also don't owe a damn thing to *anybody* other than God and each other. We're still laughing and singing and dancing over here, just in somebody else's kitchen. I think ownership of anything might be illusory anyway. It's like we can hear God saying, *Hey guys, did you really think it was the house and the money that kept you safe and warm and joyful?* I feel like a kid who finally found the courage to jump off the edge into the pool and realized, *Yes! Daddy caught me, just like he promised he would. How fun!*

Craig and I feel wide awake and very *young*. You know that feeling you had when you first got married? Like it was just you two setting off like pioneers into the big world and *anything* was possible? That's how we feel. Like newlyweds. Without a bank account to depend on, we're left with God and each other. So we get to relearn every day that God and each other are enough. We get to live on faith for a little while. The strange truth is that since we've abandoned the responsibility of providing for ourselves and given that burden to God, we feel free as birds.

Wherever You Go

Bubba is a wise man. I believe the same things about life that he does, with one important exception: Bubba taught us to *never quit*. Growing up, it was important to think twice before taking up gymnastics or the viola, because you knew you would be turning cartwheels while fiddling at your own funeral. I have a different opinion about quitting. I think that sometimes quitting is exactly the right thing to do. Quitting something that's not working requires self-awareness and courage. So Craig and I decided to go for it. We quit.

We responded to a feeling down deep in our souls, in that place that won't be ignored, that our family needed a big change. We needed cheaper, simpler, and slower. I was drowning in the details of suburban family life: the PTA meetings, birthday parties, fundraisers, thank-you notes, athletics, playdates, girls' nights out, and storytimes. I felt like a girl on a roller coaster who preferred to be pulled along gently in a red wagon. Lyme has taught me to pay attention to what I need and to honor each of the deep desires of my soul, in case God put them there as the stepping-stones toward my best life. My soul's desire is to live in a place that matches my insides. My insides are slow. I wanted to live in a place where it's okay to be slow.

I wanted time to enjoy my kids and read and write and pray and heal, not just from Lyme, but from *everything*. I wanted fewer options, less noise, fewer cars and stores and outings that require dressing nicely. I wanted more space—not walk-in-closet space, but I-can't-see-another-soul space. I wanted more empty time. I wanted to know fewer people more intimately. I wanted to go to a small-town church every Sunday morning. I wanted there to be fewer things I had to buy. Fewer meetings to miss. Less, less, *less.* I wanted *my family back.* So after we sold the house, we moved. We pulled our kids out of school, packed our bags, and rented a little house on the Chesapeake Bay in a Norman Rockwell town in which the only store is the ice cream/gossip shop. It's everything we dreamed it would be.

It's *Family.* We're a WE here. Instead of five I's, we're a WE. What little there is to do, we do together. We watch Chase stroll down to our dock with his net thrown over his shoulder like an Asian Tom Sawyer. We watch him catch *NINE SHRIMP, MOM!* and we clap and hoot and holler. We drive our golf cart over to Bubba's and Tisha's to sell Bubba the shrimp. We let Amma do the driving. She's little, but she can maneuver our golf cart like nobody's business. We giggle with Tisha while Chase and Bubba haggle over shrimp prices, finally settling on ten cents a shrimp. Bubba hands over the ninety cents, grumbling about inflation. We all know that the second we leave, he'll pour those shrimp right back into the bay.

We have roadside time-outs in cornfields. Nothing fixes a whiny road trip faster than pulling over and placing a shocked Melton bottom firmly between two stalks of corn. I smile and wave to the concerned passersby, while Tish screams, "MOMMY! YOU CAN'T JUST **DO** THIS! I'M IN THE **CORN**!!" Still, I've found more space in my day and heart to let Tish be Tish. If the girl wants to spend thirty minutes deciding which pair of wool tights to wear to the beach on a ninety-degree day, so be it.

We've got time. Time to notice how beautiful she is with a tan, how brave she is when she jumps off the dock into the bay, how gentle she is, so often, with her baby sister. I'm learning, slowly, that Tish is not just a challenging part of *my* day; she's a whole person, with her own days. Some of her days are harder than others, like mine. I'm *noticing* her more.

And Sweet *Amma*. Amma is growing up, out, and away. She gets angry fifty times a day, and she points at me in the midst of her fury and screams, "I HAS A SAD AT **YOU**, MOMMY!" And right there, in that accusation, I see that our separation has begun. Amma has learned that not only am I not the solution to all of her problems, but perhaps I'm the cause of them. So she flails and kicks on her time-out chair screaming, "I SO *FWUST-WATING*!!!!" To which I reply, "Oh, sweet girl. I couldn't agree more."

On Wednesday afternoons we sit on our front porch steps, licking popsicles and waiting for a glimpse of Craig's red truck coming down Main Street. Then I watch my babies jump up and down as Craig climbs out of the truck and prepares for their attack. I watch Craig struggle to untangle himself from their sticky little hands, so he can get to me first. I take in his suit and tie, his shiny black shoes, his cologne, and I know that over the next several days, he'll transform from business man to outdoors man. His clean-shaven face will get a little scruffier each day. The smell of cologne will be replaced by sweat and salt and sunscreen. His button-down will be replaced by nothing but dark, smooth skin and tattoos. Tattoos that mean *family*.

It's me. Something's changing inside and outside. I haven't bought a thing for months and can't think of anything I need. I haven't waxed my eyebrows or painted my nails or used a hair dryer for sixty-three days. I like figuring out what I actually look like. A little shabby—but not TOO shabby. No complaints from Craig. I read a while ago that it's not how a woman looks *for* a man that matters to him, but how she looks *at* a man. I've been testing that theory. So far, so good.

It's church. Our tiny church is a few steps from our house, so we walk every Sunday. Tish walks to church carrying her hot pink purse and tripping over her silvery glitter slippers. Fancy shoes and purses are Tish's favorite part of God.

On Easter Sunday we sat beside a teeny elderly lady who looked as if she'd been getting ready for the service since Good Friday. I admired her sculpted white curls, her tailored suit, her pale pink fingernails, and her delicate hands, which were wrapped around a snazzy pink plaid clutch. She wore a pearl necklace with matching earrings and perfectly applied cotton candy lipstick. During the service, I looked down at her ankles and noticed a blue crab peeking through her nude hose. She saw me looking and winked at me. My heart skipped a beat. I missed the entire sermon thinking about her. I've decided that dainty tattooed elderly ladies in church pews are my favorite kind of people ever. I can't wait to be one.

And it's the church bells. The first bells chime at nine, and then every three hours for the rest of the day. We can hear them from the front yard, from the dock, from the living room. I love them because they're beautiful, and because they remind me every three hours to wake up and say thank-you. Hearing those bells makes me feel like God's got his eye on our little town. Or at least our town's got its little eye on God. It feels cozy. It feels like all of us who hear the bells are in this life together.

It's the small town *attention to detail*. It's harder to pretend that people or moments are dispensable here. You have to be careful in a small town. If someone has a barking dog, or is driving too slow, you should not give the dog dirty looks or cut the slow person off. Because then you will forever be The Lady Who Gives Dogs Dirty Looks and Cuts People Off. There is no anonymity here. People are responsible for their actions. And if you don't like your neighbor, well you best find *something* you like, because nobody's going anywhere. There're just not enough folks to keep trying people out until you find one who matches you perfectly. I'm learning to practice what I preach to the kids: *you get what you get, and you don't throw a fit.*

Once, in the car, the radio station paused midsong to announce that a little boy named John had lost his dog. The dog was black with white spots and answered to the name of Rudy. Apparently John was extremely distraught. So could everyone keep an eye out and call the station if anybody saw Rudy? Then the all-call was over and the song resumed. I started crying a little. Chase heard me and said from the back seat, "It's okay, Mommy. They'll find Rudy." I told Chase that I knew they would. I was crying happy tears because I didn't know there were still places where lost puppies and heartsick little boys were worthy of interruptions.

Another time, our minister, Valerie, asked our tiny congregation for announcements. An elderly lady in the choir stood up in her shiny blue robe and held a spoon in the air. Not a special serving spoon, just a plain, metal cereal spoon. The dainty elderly choir lady said very slowly, "I think someone left this spoon at my house. If it's yours, I'd like to get it back it to you." My eyes widened and searched the sanctuary, expecting to see the knowing smiles of people tolerating this woman who was boldly spending their precious time on a single spoon. In fact, everyone was smiling earnestly at the choir lady and the spoon, including Pastor Valerie, because they were both *theirs*. The choir lady and the spoon. And they, the choir lady and the spoon, deserved to be treated with respect. And I thought, *Oh, my. I have much to learn from these people. They know that God is in the details. They know that old ladies and lost spoons are infinitely more important than time.*

It's the land. Here, there are not six degrees of separation between God's creation and our survival. Bubba introduced us to the local watermen, and we watch them take their boats out each morning to catch the fish that we eat for dinner, the fish they sell to feed their families. Chase has gone fishing with these watermen twice, and each time he's caught a week's worth of dinner. Our freezer is full of rockfish, and when Craig grills and serves it, Chase watches us chew each bite, pride puffing up his teeny chest. He's also met the local farmers and visited their farms, and as we pass by the crops, he examines them and says things like, *"The corn is looking a little short, Mom. It should be knee high by the Fourth of July. We need some rain, Mom. Rain is what we need."* Then at night he prays for rain for his farmer friends. He is starting to know the people who work the land and the water to feed America. He's learning how it *works.* That real people and real miracles put his dinner on the table.

In the absence of buildings and highways, it's easier for me to remember God's providence. Living here is a constant reminder that God made it all, and what God made is enough. Enough to feed us, to entertain us, to satisfy us. Back home all the concrete and highways and business and hyperorganization tricked me into believing that we must provide for ourselves. That we must stay very, very busy in order to keep things running. But we don't, really. We can just do our work for the day and then watch things grow.

It's the water. There's a glass door at the back of our house that frames the bay inside of it, and I've watched each member of our family stop in his tracks at that door, look out at the water, and sigh. Even Amma sighs at that door. It's as if our bodies are designed to stop, relax, and appreciate the water. There's a lot of sighing going on here. Tish lies on the dock, the sun lightening her golden brown hair, the blue water and sky swallowing her up. She says, "AH. THIS IS MY YIFE." She means "this is the life," but I don't correct her.

Sometimes, early in the morning, I sneak out to the back porch with my coffee and C. S. Lewis and listen to the bay wake up. I never get much reading done, because I find myself silently repeating, "thank you, thank you, thank you." Something about water helps me feel grateful. Whether it's a glass of ice water, a warm tub, or the bay.

In the evening I stand in the kitchen, cutting local veggies while Craig chases the kids around the house. They laugh until they can't stand anymore, so they flop down and roll on the kitchen floor, holding their bellies. I look out the back window to the water and sing along to my country music. I realize that my life matches my music now. This is all I needed—just a safe, pretty place to let my faith, family, and bangs grow.

There You Are

B ut then I learned that a pretty place wasn't all I needed.

Here's what I discovered in my six months by the water: The bay is beautiful, but not as lovely as my friends Brooke and Amy. The morning sounds of the bay comfort me, but Casey's twinkly eyes and a hug from Jen comfort me even more. Watching the kids splash in the bay is exhilarating, but not as refreshing as watching them squeal as they greet Jess at the door. God made some beautiful things—and the bay is one of them—but I'm certain that women were his best work. There is no substitute on God's Green Earth for girlfriends.

I've never felt particularly good at friendship. Friendship's demands—like remembering important dates, answering the phone, and navigating group dynamics—don't come easy to me. I have a reclusive side and a Sister. These two things make friendship hard to need. Maybe they just make it harder for me to *notice* how much I need friends.

Still, I've managed to keep a small group of best friends from college. They take incredible care of each other and make it appear so effortless. I always felt well loved by them, but also a few steps removed. I could never be *all in* the way they were with each other. I kept one foot out, mostly because I have a hard time feeling like an essential part of any group. Groups are hard. But also because everything for which they relied on each other—advice, support, a shoulder to cry on, a shopping partner—I already had in Sister. So I never really thought I *needed* them. But after a few months in my new town, it became clear that it was going to be very hard to make new friends and impossible to replace those I already had. Marriage and parenting become extra hard without friends with whom to discuss how wonderful and *hard* they are.

So Craig and I started talking about what this meant for us. Our marriage is a twisty, mapless journey. We try one thing, then try another. We decide what works and what doesn't. We get to know each other better with each new try, and then we fix things for each other and try not to lose our patience. We try to be tireless with each other's hearts. We are slowly and painstakingly learning how to do this well.

In the end, we decided to move back to our friends in the suburbs. It had become clear that I *needed* to. As a recovering everything, loneliness is dangerous territory for me. I don't know how it works, but being plugged into others, instead of allowing myself to float untethered like a satellite, is one of the keys to my sobriety. And there was one lonely night in our teeny town when I glanced at the wine bottle on top of the fridge for a *couple of seconds* too long. That scared the bejesus out of me. And Craig is wise enough to know that if I go down, *the whole fam damily goes down.*

So we moved into a neighborhood where four of my very best friends live. We walk to each other's houses, and our little ones go to school together. When Craig calls and says he's going to be home late, I call my girls and say *come over right away*. Our million collective littles run around the house while we mamas talk and drink Diet Coke out of wine glasses, because Manal's mom said it tastes better that way. It *does*. We make nine frozen pizzas, and I burn most of them and Gena looks at me above the chaos and says, *"I can't believe this. I can't believe how lucky we are. Twenty years. We're mamas together."*

And when I look at Gena—all of the *Genas* flash before me:

I see her in the sparkly formal gown she wore to a dance during her freshman year in college. Then I see her in her black graduation gown, holding her diploma. Next I see her walking down the aisle toward Zach in a gorgeous white wedding gown. Then she appears in the pale blue gown she wore in the hospital as she held her first baby, Tyler. Finally, I smile as I remember the sassy black and white number she wore to the spectacular party that marked their ten-year anniversary.

And with goosebumps covering my arms and legs, I think— *we are growing up together,* like Sisters do. We're *friends*. I know we're friends because I need you, I don't understand why. I'm just grateful that I do.

As I turn to watch Gena's little girls chasing mine up the stairs in their Snow White dresses, I think, *Yep*. I found my *small town*. My *water*. My small town and my water are my *family and friends*. And for the first time, I'm all in.

Sometimes you have to leave to discover that you left everything you needed back home. Is our life back home perfect? *Hell no*. But I have finally learned that I am not going to be perfectly happy anywhere. If I live by the water, I will miss the suburbs. If I live in the mountains, I will miss the water. If I watch *House Hunters International,* I will miss Costa Rica. And I've never even been to Costa Rica.

I've done the experiment. I've moved six times in eight years to very different places, desperately seeking peace and joy. And I still haven't found what I'm lookin' for. Parenting, life, friendship, marriage: they are not hard for me *because I'm in the wrong place;* they're just *hard*. So I am finally willing to accept that there is no geographic place that offers perfect peace. Because, as Bubba likes to say, *wherever you go, there you are.*

I think one of the keys to happiness is accepting that I am never going to be perfectly happy. Life is uncomfortable. So I might as well get busy loving the people around me. I'm going to stop trying so hard to decide whether they are the "right people" for me and just take deep breaths and love my neighbors. I'm going to take care of my friends. I'm going to find peace in the 'burbs. I'm going to quit chasing happiness long enough to notice it smiling right at me.

Healing Is Listening

We Can Do Hard Things
We Belong to Each Other
Love Wins

*H*ello, *blank page.* We meet again. Each blank page is like a new day, a gift that comes with responsibility. *What will I make of you? You scare me, but I love you.* It's appropriate that *scared* and *sacred* are virtually the same word, because those two walk hand in hand.

The blank page feels especially scary and sacred today because I've decided to respond to a question that's been asked of me with some frequency: *"Glennon," people say, "you were a bulimic for twenty years, an alcoholic and smoker for ten, and a drug user for five. You quit all four cold turkey, without working the twelve steps. That's unusual. And I notice you're quite skinny. Are you sure you're better?"*

Better is a troublesome word for me. *Better* suggests increased value, and I think I was worth exactly the same when I was a fall-down drunk as I am now: a sober, loving, creative wife, mother, sister, daughter, and friend.

I prefer the word *healing* to the word *better*. To me, *healing* means aligning myself—my mind, body, and soul—with the rhythm of the world. It means relaxing into the way things are, floating with the current instead of desperately trying to swim against it. *Healing* means surrendering to and following the world's truest rules, the rules created by God.

When discussing God with people of different faiths, *Love* is a good word to use because most people believe that Love can be trusted. It has been said that the opposite of Love is Hate, or perhaps apathy. Yet, I'm fairly certain that the opposite of Love is Fear. I think the root of all evil is fear.

Love and Fear are opposing voices, opposing ways to live, opposing platforms on which to make daily decisions, view the world, and build a life. The battle between Love and Fear is at the heart of my healing, my recovery, my progress toward heaven. My *better*.

There are two voices in my head. One jumps up and down, waves its arms, clamors for my attention, and generally annoys the hell (heaven) out of me. That voice is Fear. For twenty years, I heard only the voice of Fear, so I believed fear was the truth. I thought Fear was *my* voice. Here is what Fear said to me, all day, every day:

There is not enough for you. Hurry. Grab food, grab money, grab attention and fame and validation and praise, and hold on tight. These things might never come your way again. The more for her, the less for you. Get what you can while you can and hoard it, hide it.

Actually, forget it. Take nothing. You don't deserve anything. And stay away from people. If anyone really knew you, they'd be horrified. There is something very, very wrong with you. Look at your life, your body, your face! Humiliating. Grotesque. You are beyond repair. You have nothing to offer. Life has nothing to offer either—nothing you deserve, at least.

246

Life is terrible and soul crushing to weaklings like you. You will not be able to handle it. Stay quiet and hide until the end.

I followed every one of Fear's directions for nearly twenty years.

Then, when I got pregnant, I was certain it would end badly, because Fear told me that an unhappy ending was exactly what a girl like me deserved. But it didn't end badly; it ended miraculously. I found myself holding a beautiful, perfect baby boy—a completely undeserved gift. And a kind, giving, gorgeous man decided to marry me. *ME*. And after the decades of pain I caused my friends and my family, they still surrounded me and loved my little family and wanted to help us.

It occurred to me, Could Fear be wrong? I said, *Are you a LIAR, Fear? Is there another way to live? Is there another voice?*

As soon as I figured out that Fear wasn't my only voice, it faded into the background. Something else emerged. This presence had been sitting quietly and solidly, with a voice as tall and deep and wide as a redwood tree. This voice, I understood quickly, was Love. I call him Jesus, and in my mind's eye he sits, smiling softly, still as a rock, and *knowing*.

I couldn't hear Love because I was never quiet enough. Fear does not want you to hear what is said in the quiet, because Love and Truth are there. So Fear yells and jumps relentlessly, like a desperate actor on an infomercial. But Love is patient. Love waits until you are ready to tune out Fear. When I was ready, I could hear Love speak.

Love said:

Stop grabbing, sweetheart. Stop holding your breath. Breathe. There is enough. I've created an abundance of acceptance, attention, recognition, joy, peace, money, energy, clothes, food. I will never leave you without enough. And there is nothing to be afraid of. No feeling, no circumstance, no person. These things come and they go, and you can live through them, without running, hiding, numbing, or hurting another of my children. And did you know this, my angel? There has never been anything wrong with you—not one day in your life. You are exactly who you were meant to be, right now, as you are. You are not to be ashamed. You punish yourself, but you have no reason to be punished. You have done just fine. No one wants you punished. You can stop that now. You are free.

Now listen carefully, because this is important: When you were born, I put a piece of myself in you. Like an indestructible, brilliant diamond, I placed a part of me inside of you. That part of you—the very essence of you, in fact—is me; it is Love, it is perfect, and it is untouchable. No one can take it, and you can't give it away. It is the deepest, truest part of you, the part that will someday return to me. You are Love. You cannot be tarnished by anything you've done or that anyone else has done to you. Everyone carries this piece of me—this perfect Love. You are all a part of me, and I am part of you, and you are a part of each other. The essence of each of you is Love.

Your first job is to know that: to float and swim in that knowledge, to believe that the Love, the spirit, the God in you and in everyone, is equally brilliant and unmarred. Your second job is to help other people know about their brilliance, their essence, their perfection, their core—which is perfect Love. When they speak to you from their fear—speak past their fear and directly to their love. Their Love will step forward eventually. It's one of my Rules. Be patient.

Do not worry. Come out of hiding, because you have these two jobs to do: be still and know, and then help others know. Since you carry me with you, you know what to do. You always know the next right thing. Be still and ask yourself, *What would love do?* Then get quiet, and I, I, inside of you, will tell you. You will take the next right step. Love will reveal itself one step at a time, the whole way home. Along the way, accept my blessings and give them away freely. You are worthy of giving and receiving. Believe. You are new, every moment, new. Your time, your energy, your mind, the people who come into your life—they are all gifts from me and they are infinite. They belong to you and to everyone else.

In one of my favorite books, *Traveling Mercies,* Anne Lamott quotes William Blake: "We are put on this Earth to learn to endure the beams of Love." Enduring Love burns at first. The Love voice is nearly impossible to accept, because it seems too good to be true.

But I really wanted Love to be true, so I decided to give her a chance. Love promised that I didn't have to run or hide or numb myself from life anymore. Love told me that I could live through my feelings with her help. I decided to test these promises one at a time. I stopped smoking, drinking, bingeing, puking, and drugging, all at once. I read somewhere that *"the truth will set you free—but it will piss you off first."* That certainly proved to be accurate. I shook and sweated and *cursed* Love for two weeks. Eventually, though, I stopped shaking. The world became brighter and clearer. I saw my first sober sunrise in decades.

After I gave birth to Chase, I felt myself loving my baby, giving myself to him, caring for his needs, as if I had something to offer. I wasn't sure I actually had something to offer him, but it felt like

I had to pretend I did. So I just pretended. But he responded to my offering by loving and needing me. *Me*. And I knew he wasn't pretending because he was just a baby and babies haven't heard fear yet. The love between Chase and me became very, very real. So I tried loving my husband too. Loving Craig, a real live grown-up, was harder—but he responded too. I could tell that he was starting to love me back.

These two people, they needed me. *Me*. If two such good, kind, full people needed and wanted and loved me, could I really be so worthless? Suddenly it seemed that there might be parts of life that were beautiful and good and that were meant for *ME*. I became even more suspicious of the bastard from whom I'd been taking orders for twenty years.

So I started listening harder. I looked closely at people and nature and read books about God and Love. Without all the bingeing and purging, my skin cleared up and my cheeks, bloated from years of broken blood vessels, flattened out. As the tobacco loosened from my lungs, I was able to take deep breaths again. I needed those deep breaths. I felt sad and terrified and angry, and with nothing to dull those feelings, I learned to just *let feelings be*—because eventually they pass. I learned that all things pass; that life is hard to endure but not impossible. I discovered that after the enduring, if you choose not to run away, there are prizes. Those prizes are wisdom and dignity. I learned that Love and I, We could do hard things.

Next, I tested out Love's claim that I had nothing to be ashamed of. That promise was the hardest to swallow, but since Love had not lied to me yet, I had to try. I started writing and publishing all of the secret thoughts and feelings that Fear had promised I'd be shunned and despised for having. I published my insides *on the Internet*. The Internet is read by many, *many* people, you know. Many people whose anonymity allows them to be especially vicious. Still, I did not become despised. Very few were vicious. It turned out that sharing my secret self made me more beloved by others than I'd ever been in my life. Then I saw that when I allowed Love to set me free through my writing, my readers decided to set themselves free too. Another miracle: people wrote, *not* to say that they were disgusted or horrified by me, but that they saw themselves—their own battles and triumphs—in my experiences.

And I realized the secret of my writing is this: the voice I use to write is not really my voice. It's Love's voice. I say what she says; I write what she prompts me to write. And that's why you recognize the voice. Because you have the same voice inside you. My love voice speaks directly to yours. We are the same. At our core, we are exactly the same. We are Love. The heart rejoices when it hears the truth. Namaste—*the divine light in me recognizes and honors the divine light in you.*

Next, I decided to test Love's claims about giving. Craig and I gave away all of our money, twice. Once to an orphanage and again to our mortgage company. With nothing, we were happier than we'd ever been. That's the thing about losing *it* all. You realize you're fine without *it*. For the first time in our lives, we felt secure. It was a miracle. When you give *it* all away—the stuff—you learn that it is impossible to lose whatever it is that you cannot live without. Love was right. The thing you need is unshakable, untakable. What you need is not in things, it's in you. It's Love.

The more fiercely I believe what Love says and the more boldly I live out her promises, the healthier and stronger and realer I become. So, for me, it's not a question of better. It's about a daily choice: the constant battle to listen to Love and silence Fear. Of course, even though I choose Love daily, I can still hear the reverberations of Fear's voice, like a bell that keeps echoing even after it's been stilled. Right now I am neither Fear nor Love, but the one who chooses between them. However, I have a feeling that after years of choosing Love, after decades of ignoring Fear and *tuning into Love,* I will *turn into Love*. I pray that she and I will become one, that eventually all the words that come out of my mouth will be her words. And that when I slip into the arms of God, it will be as if there were no break at all in our eternal conversation. When I die, God will look at me and say, *"Now where were we, Darling?"*

But for now, I feel myself rising, rising, rising. I am free. I am *healing*.

It Will Be Beautiful

For years, people have asked me where my passion to adopt originated. I've tried to explain it so many different ways, fumbling, offering statistics and scriptures about the need for orphan care, ultimately becoming flustered and defensive. None of it rang true to me. All the *reasons* were there, just not the *real reason*. The real reason was down far too deep to pull up and describe with words.

Then one day I read *Pillars of the Earth* by Ken Follett. In it, there is a character named Tom, a craftsman of little means, who is obsessed with the idea of building a cathedral to God. In his quest to realize this goal, he squanders his savings, puts his family through hell, and spends the prime of his life searching, planning, and dreaming this impossible dream. After twenty years, Tom finds himself in front of a man with the means to help. The man asks him one simple but loaded question. *Why? Why do you want to build this cathedral so badly?* Tom hesitates for a moment and says, *Because it will be beautiful.* My heart soared when I read that line. Yes. Because it will be beautiful. *That* is the truest answer to the question I've been asked for so many years. *Glennon, why do you want to adopt?* Because it will be beautiful.

I want to adopt to live the belief that We Belong to Each Other—that we are one human family—to look beyond my backyard and to welcome one of God's children as my own.

Because to join in communion and grief and redemption with every mother who has wanted desperately to raise her own baby but lacked the resources—well, it's the most beautiful thing I can imagine. And that's what I do. I think of the most beautiful thing I can imagine and then try to do that thing. It's an interesting but difficult way to live.

Craig and I tried to adopt for years. We spent our days and evenings on the phone, Internet, and each other's nerves trying to adopt internationally. Each time we got close, the dreaded background check arrived, and agency after agency rejected us because of my checkered record and status as a recovering alcoholic.

I cried myself to sleep many nights, while Craig squeezed me tight and prayed that God would either open an adoption door or take away the desperation in my heart. Then I'd wake up early to start the whole obsessive process over again. During one interview, as the social worker asked us questions about the past and we answered them honestly, we could actually hear her voice become more distant and cold. I said, "I don't think she's going to give us a baby, do you?" Craig shook his head and admitted that he wanted to stop doing interviews altogether because he was afraid they'd take away the kids we already had. I constantly doubted my worth as a mother, because we were repeatedly told in so many words that these babies were better off in orphanages than in my home. It was humbling, and it shook my faith.

Then, in August, we found some hope at an agency that facilitated adoptions from Guatemala. The social worker told us that they would find a way to bring us a baby from their orphanage. The agency sent us pictures of the little ones, and I fell in love. While our paperwork was being processed, I spent my days mentally planning and daydreaming. I knew our baby would be a little girl, and I knew her name would be Maria. I have no idea where this information originated, so I assumed it was from God. I never told anyone that I knew she would be named Maria, because people can only be expected to take so much. But I knew it. There was a country song out at the time called "My Maria," and I would drive around, belting out the lyrics and fantasizing about how Craig, Chase, Tish, Maria, and I would dance to "My Maria" in front of our family and friends at Maria's coming-home party.

Eventually, we got a phone call from the agency. Craig took the call, and then he told me gently that the agency had decided we were too much of a risk. The door to Guatemala was officially closed. I sat on the floor, stunned and devastated. Chase walked in while I sobbed, and he looked at Craig and said, "Why?" Craig said, "She's just sad, honey. Mommy's just sad." Months passed and I pulled myself together, reasonably enough.

Christmas morning came, and after the flurry of excitement and gifts, we all rested into the day. Bubba fell asleep and Sister and Tisha slid into the kitchen to start breakfast. I flopped onto the couch and congratulated myself for pulling off another Christmas. Craig snuggled next to me and handed me one last gift that he had hidden away. I smiled and opened it, and when all of the paper was removed, I was holding a scrapbook, hand-made by Craig. In a square plastic frame on the cover was a little girl's smiling face. The girl looked about seven years old. She had deep brown eyes, long, mocha curls, and a brilliant smile. Underneath her picture, Craig had written out her name in letter stickers: *Maria Renee.*

After we found out we wouldn't be allowed to bring a baby home from Guatemala, Craig called the agency to ask if he could sponsor a child there, in honor of me and of our dream. The woman at the orphanage said they had *just the little girl for us.* Her name was Maria, she said. She sent Craig pictures of Maria and her orphanage home, and Craig put them together in a scrapbook for me so I'd have something to hold on Christmas morning.

I bawled 'til I couldn't see. Bubba woke up and became alarmed. Everyone stared. I didn't care. I have never in my life felt the presence of God more strongly than I did at that moment, sitting with that scrapbook in my lap and my husband beside me. I actually felt God saying, "I *was* watching, and I *was* speaking. You were right, there *is* a Maria for you. Here she is."

Since I couldn't speak, I left my family and walked into my bedroom, found my journal, and brought it back to the family room. I opened it and showed them page after page where I'd doodled "Maria Melton" like a lovesick teenager.

We fell more deeply in love with Maria during the next year. We sent her gifts and letters that my mom translated into Spanish for us. We told her that God loved her very much and so did we, and we explained that we prayed for her and for her friends every night. We asked Chase's birthday party guests to donate money instead of gifts, and we sent the money to Maria so that she could throw a birthday party for herself that year. The orphanage told us that the money went so far that Maria was able to invite another orphanage to her party too, and that they all played with piñatas and balloons for the first time in their lives.

We got a letter last year announcing that Maria had finally been adopted by a family in the States. The odds had been against her. We had been told that the likelihood that Maria would find a forever home was slim to none, but we know that with God, nothing is impossible.

A few months later, we decided to try again. Chase wasn't so sure about this plan. When I told him we were going to start a Vietnamese adoption he said, *I don't know, Mom. We don't seem to be very good at this. Maybe we should just adopt a highway.* I probably should have listened, because a few months later we found out that the Vietnamese didn't want us either. Craig and I decided that God was clearly telling us to *let go.* So we tried, but we couldn't. One day in the car, we decided that we would just start another home study, an intense and lengthy interview with a social worker, without an agency or country that would accept us. We hoped that once we stepped out in faith, our next step would be revealed. We already had a social worker who was ready to get us started and the money we needed in the bank. Our hope and energy were renewed. Once again, I started picturing Chase and Tish holding their new sibling.

When we arrived home from that exciting car ride, I went through the mail and saw a letter from the Guatemalan agency that had helped us try to adopt. The letter was from *Maria's* orphanage. It began like this: *"This is one of the toughest times I've seen at our home in Guatemala. My heart breaks to think of the children we've had to turn away. Toddlers roaming among piles of garbage, six-year-olds begging for food, ten-year-old girls caring for infant siblings on their own."* The letter went on to describe a four-year-old girl named Marielos whom police had brought to the orphanage after her mother's boyfriend raped her repeatedly. She spent her first week there *"either speechless or sobbing."* The director wrote that she *"stayed up with Marielos many nights, holding her tightly as she cried softly."* Next she described the miraculous way Marielos began to heal in the arms of her *"special mother."* But then she reported that due to lack of funds, the orphanage was being forced to turn away traumatized children like Marielos every day. The letter was a request for small donations that, combined, would keep the orphanage running. My head spun when I saw the amount that they needed: it was almost exactly the amount that Craig and I had saved for the adoption.

I sensed a voice that was a calmer version of my own suggest something like, *Here we are. Now what do you want more? Do you really want to help my orphans, or do you really want an adopted child? There might be a difference.* I stood in the kitchen, stunned and sweating. The suggestion continued, *You've been begging for an invitation from me, and you're holding it.*

I considered not telling Craig about the letter and the voice. Not because I was worried he'd think I was crazy, which is what I usually worry about, but because I was afraid he would know the right thing to do, and then *he'd want to do it.* But I told him anyway. And he listened, and he read the letter, and then got very quiet. He said, "You know, if we do this, it means we won't have any adoption money left." I said, "Yes, it would mean giving that away for this, I guess." We went to bed early that night and didn't speak about it again. We were well aware that we were walking on holy ground.

I sent one e-mail to Craig the next morning, telling him that I wasn't able to make this decision because I was too blinded by my own desire for a baby. I wanted him to decide. That night he came home and he said quietly that he was positive that the money belonged to the orphanage. He had sent our adoption fund, which was two-thirds of the total amount they needed to keep the orphanage afloat, and our entire savings account. Next: Lots more quiet, a few tears, and then just awe . . . and peace.

Peace, for me, usually lasts about twenty minutes. At this point, one might assume that I finally decided that it was time to leave it all well enough alone and focus on the blessings right in front of me. That's really not my style.

When Sister was in Rwanda working with the International Justice Mission, she spent every Sunday at a Missionaries of Charity orphanage, holding babies. For hours upon hours, she held four children at a time as they climbed her legs and back and touched her face, desperate for touch, affection, connection. Sister told us that there were children there who desperately needed to be adopted.

Craig and I agreed that *this must* be the invitation for which we'd been waiting so long. We began again. We spent six months jumping through hoop after exhausting hoop trying to get approved to adopt a Rwandan baby. We were urged on by "sign" after "sign" that we were on the right track: a favorable home study, an FBI clearance (!), our final paperwork. One of the Sisters who ran the orphanage even told Sister that she knew which baby was ours—a five-month-old little boy. We named him Hills. Rwanda is called the *Land of a Thousand Hills,* and we thought Hills an appropriate name to describe the journey we took to find him. My name, Glennon, means valley, or resting place between the hills. I thought that our little man was going to have a wonderful life with us, but not one without challenges. I wanted to be his valley, his resting place between the Hills of Life.

We were waiting on one piece of paper. Just one, and we could send our entire "dossier" to Rwanda and take our place in line. But one morning I woke up to a 911 message from Sister. She said that Rwanda, without notice, was terminating adoptions. Any family whose completed paperwork was not *in Rwanda by the end of the day* was unqualified to adopt. I was stunned. I was furious. Our *baby.* Craig and I looked at each other and said, *Oh . . . hellllllll NO.*

We dropped the girls off at a friend's house at six in the morning and drove to Washington, D.C. We found the Rwandan embassy. We walked in, introduced ourselves, and kindly explained that we were not leaving until our final paperwork was signed and we were grandfathered in to the adoption system.

Then we turned toward the tiny embassy lobby and saw three other anxious-looking couples already sitting there. They were there for the same reason we were. They had all flown in from Texas when they heard the news. They were staging a sit-in too. We started teary introductions and I turned to one gentleman, Mark, and said, *Hello, I'm Glennon. This is my son, Chase.* Chase reached out his little hand, and as Mark shook it, his eyes started watering. I felt concerned. Mark asked me if he could take a picture of Chase to send to his wife. I felt more concerned but consented. After Mark sent the picture, he explained that his family's adoption journey began when his wife lost their baby boy, Chase, to a miscarriage. When he sent Chase's picture to his wife, he included a message that said, *Honey, it's going to be okay. I just got to the embassy and Chase is here.*

It was that kind of day.

The Rwandan embassy is the size of a large walk-in closet, and as time went on, it became increasingly awkward for everyone. The people in charge told us again and again, politely, that there was nothing that they could do, that this was a government order, that we were wasting our time and we should leave. We did leave, but came back with lunch for ourselves and all the embassy workers. We politely explained that we couldn't go because leaving would mean leaving our babies. And so we all sat and laughed and cried together for twelve hours. The office was supposed to close at 5:00 p.m. At 4:45, I felt the tears coming. The end was near. At 5:15, a Rwandan woman walked down the stairs and handed a piece of paper to each of us. The paper signified that our four families had been grandfathered into the adoption system. We were going to get our babies. She said, *You came. You came for the children, so we did this for you.*

That was an important lesson: SHOW UP. You never know what might happen.

We were done. There was nothing left to do but wait for our travel orders and decorate the nursery and celebrate with friends. We did all of those things. Then two months later we got a letter declaring that Rwandan adoptions were closed indefinitely. It was over and done. Hills was not coming home. He was not ours, after all.

Tish wrote this poem recently:

> *Woood you still love the uuniverse if the sky wernt blue?*
> *I wood still love the uuniverse, woood you?*

I had to think about that for a long while. But I decided, yes. Yes, I would. I would still love the stupid uuniverse.

No, I didn't get what I wanted. I didn't get my baby, and with my deteriorating health, it's not likely I ever will. It is official: I did not get the life I wanted. I did not become an adoptive mother, I did not get to travel and hold the one God meant for me, I did not get to send the Christmas card that would say, *Happy Holidays, Love, The Melton Pot!*

But when your miracle doesn't happen the way you planned, it becomes important to look for peripheral miracles. Peripheral miracles are those that aren't directly in front of you. They're not the one on which you've been *so damned focused*. You have to turn your head to see peripheral miracles.

I was so focused on building my little teeny altar to God, my head down, sweating, cursing, stressing, furiously working with broken tools, that I missed the city of cathedrals he was busy building around me. When I was finally able to lift my head, I saw the community of people who had rallied around me and my family. *My family*—my three healthy children and strong husband. My baby, Amma, who may have never *been* if we'd adopted. And I saw that the very vehicle I had used to vent about my pain and confusion about the adoption and my health—my blog—had become a community of thousands and thousands of people who were *learning* from my journey.

So like an owl, I kept turning my head. And I saw Tara and Isaac, whom I met at the embassy that day, holding their son, Zane. They *got* their baby. And I saw Mark and Chelsea, the couple who lost their Chase, holding their Rwandan baby, Gabe. And I saw Sister's son, Bobby, whom I'll hold every day of my life but *never have to send to college.* And I looked down and saw a book deal in my hands, and request after request from people to have me come speak—to speak to them about hope and love. They didn't care that my dream didn't come true. They just cared that I was true to my dream. That I never gave up hope. That I shared it all. And that even though I didn't get what I wanted, I could see—I could see—that I'd gotten what I needed. I'd tried to adopt one, to give hope to *one little one,* and instead, God gave me thousands to speak to about my senseless, relentless hope.

There are only two lives we might live: our dream or our destiny. Sometimes they are one in the same, and sometimes they're not. Often our dreams are just a path to our destinies. My dream was to be an adoptive mother, but my destiny is to mother my three children, to be a wife, sister, friend, and daughter, and to speak hope boldly to you. My destiny is to remind you to look up from the castles you're building in the sand long enough to notice the cathedrals that God's building all around you—without you, without your sweat, without your tears, without your consent. While you dream your dreams, he's busy building your destiny. And there is as much beauty in your destiny as there was in your dream. Let go and believe that *whatever it is, it will be beautiful.**

---

*You'll be glad to know that we have, in fact, successfully adopted a highway. Our highway is going to shine like the damn yellow brick road.

By God,
There Will Be Dancing

I am sitting in a quiet bedroom with God. We are alone—the two of us. I am perched on the edge of a four-poster bed and my legs are dangling off the side. God is in a rocking chair across the room and she's knitting. God knits, it turns out. She also rides a Harley, but never while knitting.

I am pissed at God, so I'm glaring at her while she rocks and knits.

She won't ask me what's wrong. I'm waiting for her to ask. I'm dying for her to ask. I sigh. I breathe as deeply and loudly and with as much angst as possible.

Nothing from her. Nothing disturbs her peace, nothing breaks her concentration. She is not curious.

So I just start.

I'm going to stay sick, aren't I? You're not going to heal me, are you? And I'll never have another baby, will I? And my marriage. What about my marriage? Is that going to crumble too? You're going to leave me sick and empty-armed and struggling, aren't you? Aren't you? I know you are.

Please fix it. If you don't, that's it for us. I'm not kidding. I'll quit trying not to be a jerk. I'll quit writing. I'll quit talking to you and caring about other people and smiling so much. I'll spend all my money on fancy makeup and couches and I'll spend all my time watching Real Housewives of Orange County. *No.* Housewives of NEW JERSEY. *Take* that. *I'm serious. Friendship with you is too exhausting. I'm going to have to quit you, based on principle and utter confusion. If you don't pull through for me this time, it's atheism for me.* Atheism. *I'm so serious.*

God keeps knitting. Then she smiles and holds her stitch for a moment. She looks up at me with her soft crinkly eyes and she says:

Honey. You are so angry. I understand. I love you so much. Would you like me to stop knitting so that we can talk about all of this?

I think for a minute and look at the knitting in her lap. I gaze at the part that's done. It's breathtaking. All blue and green and hot pink and gold and silver. At first the colors seem to swirl wildly but then, suddenly, I recognize a pattern. The pattern is me. I am beautiful. Swirly, wild, and beautiful.

No, I say. Don't stop. Keep knitting.

Because she is knitting my life, of course. *I* am what her hands are working on. And I want her to concentrate. I still trust her.

God? I say. I'm going to dance. While you knit, I'm just going to dance.

God looks up one last time and says:

That's all I've ever wanted you to do, Sweetheart. You dance and I'll keep knitting. It's going to be beautiful, Honey. I promise.

Acknowledgments

Thank you, family and friends, for continuing to read my life story through all the plot twists and for being certain that it would end well. Thank you, Monkees, for helping me create my second home and for living there with me. Thank you to the Monkee See—Monkee Do Board of Directors—Allison, Amanda, Amy, Lou, and Liz—you are warriors for love. To Trena Keating, Sally Wofford-Girand, and Jill Gillett—thank you for believing and for so strongly and skillfully encouraging the rest of the world to believe too. To Amy, for your faith and sweat. And to my Scribner family, especially Whitney Frick—editor, friend, Monkee. We did it! We really did it, didn't we?

Sister-maktub. Thank GOD.

Momastery and
Monkee See—Monkee Do

Glennon Doyle Melton founded Momastery.com in 2009 as a part of her healing process. Momastery emerged from the idea that motherhood is like a monastery: it's a sacred place, apart from the world, where a seeker can figure out what matters and catch glimpses of God. Momastery was created to be a safe haven, a gathering place for an online order of irreverent monks. It is a place to practice living bigger, bolder, and truer on this earth. Please visit www.momastery.com to learn more.

The overflow of generosity and compassion at Momastery became Monkee See—Monkee Do, where we acknowledge the needs in our communities and we do something about them. Our work—including our revolutionary "Love Flash Mobs"—exemplifies Mother Teresa's philosophy that we can do no great things, only small things with great love. We have learned that by harnessing the power of a filled-up community, small gifts can make a tremendous impact—on givers' hearts and on the world around us. For more information, please visit www.mon keeseemonkeedo.org.

Interested in self help, spiritual and above all inspirational books?

Then join us at

WellPenguin

the exclusive Penguin facebook club for anyone who is curious about life.

- Put questions to our expert authors
- Download free wellbeing podcasts
- Enter our exciting monthly competitions
- Share your views and opinions
- Test yourself with our exclusive quizzes
- Be the first to discover about the next WellPenguin release

www.facebook.com/WellPenguin